brandspa

Phil and Dixie

Practice spreading delight and don't keep it to yourself

Allen Gorrie

Pre-release praise for
Briefs for Building Better Brands

"Allan Gorman has made a monumental contribution to the body of marketing wisdom with his brilliant *Briefs for Building Better Brands*. Not only is his book chock full of insightful information, but it is presented with warmth and clarity. I believe the book should be mandatory reading for anyone vaguely connected with creating a brand that lasts."

—JAY CONRAD LEVINSON
Author: *Guerrilla Marketing* series of books
Over 14 million sold, now in 39 languages

"Allan Gorman has a way with words which makes his advice on brand building easy to take and easy to swallow. You can learn something new and useful on every page."

—AL RIES, Ries & Ries
Best selling author of 11 marketing books, including:
Positioning—The Battle for Your Mind

"Turns buzz words like 'brand building' into something that has real meaning. He cuts to the essence of a marketing problem and then suggests solutions that work."

—DENNIS PETERS, Principal, Heavybag Media

"If you've got a brand or you dream about one, you owe it to yourself to read this book. *Briefs for Building Better Brands* is right on the money—insightful, practical, action stimulating, easy to consume, and definitely worth the time to digest."

—KAREN POST, The Branding Diva
National Speaker, Author: *Brain Tattoo*

"Allan Gorman not only understands branding, he knows how to make it understandable. No jargon, no hype, just simple common sense."

—GAYLE TURNER, Principal, Beckett & Beckett
Nationally recognized speaker
on the subject of brand for *Adweek* Conferences

"Where others are trying to force themselves to think outside the box, Gorman wants you to understand exactly 'what's in the box,' then punch through it to the other side. He ratchets up your level of comprehension to a newfound sense of clarity. From there, it's a skate to success, and the experience is wonderful. His approach to branding is infectious."

—TOM JONES, Beckwith Bay Communications

"Companies of all sizes need brand power to attract customers and succeed in business. Allan is a master at explaining how to build a brand creatively and effectively."

—LIZ LYNCH, President, Consult Ad Hoc Inc.
Author: 102 *Secrets to Smarter Networking*

"I have a litmus test regarding marketing books. They have to move me into action. A good one pulls me out of my easy chair and back to my computer where I start to apply the ideas I've learned. Allan's *Briefs for Building Better Brands* is such a book. There are practical, actionable ideas on every page. If you're serious about attaining marketing leadership for your brand, this book is a great place to start."

—ROBERT MIDDLETON, Action Plan Marketing
Marketing Coach, Author: *More Clients Newsletter*

"A brand is a hard financial asset. A good brand can be the most valuable asset a company owns. If you want such a valuable asset read this book."

—JEFFREY J. FOX
Best selling author: *How To Become a Rainmaker*

"Allan is as savvy a veteran as Madison Avenue can produce. He's seen it all and has an uncanny knack for simplifying the steps you need to take to realize market leadership. He knows what works, and what doesn't. In addition to this book, he should be in your office tomorrow if you're serious about competing more effectively."

—ELIOT PHILLIPS, Lippincott Mercer

"Who'd have thought marketing and branding could be so much fun? Allan Gorman's new 'little book,' as he humbly dubs it, is little only in the sense that it doesn't set a record for number of pages—but what a powerful, well-written, and—yes, entertaining!—little book it is! Allan's style is conversational, witty, and sometimes just plain funny. No doubt you'll have your own personal favorite among the more than a dozen essays in this little gem, but I've yet to narrow my choice to just one. A rare combination of business insights and wit to be read and re-read!"

—LINDA C. ROONEY, MIRM, CSP
President, Advantage Builder Services, L.L.C.

"*Briefs for Building Better Brands* is a treasure trove of well-written and savvy branding and marketing strategies that will help your business to rise above the norm and get noticed in a big way."

—DON GABOR, Conversation Arts Media
Best selling author:
How to Start a Conversation and Make Friends

"The toolset he'll put in your hands will enable you to turn your business into a fine-tuned marketing success machine."
—GARY WATSON, Vice President, IC&C, Inc.

"*Briefs for Building Better Brands* is one of the better business books I've read recently. Gorman brings an insight that identifies marketing problems many people are unaware of. He offers no-nonsense, easy-to-follow solutions. *Briefs for Building Better Brands* is critical material for anyone in the business of moving products and services."
—MICHAEL A. SISTI, Principal, Sisti & Others
Former Vice President of Marketing
Blue Cross/Blue Shield of Rhode Island

"If Allan were a coach in the NFL, he'd dissect each game and then take the team back to the basics. He doesn't perfect bad ideas—he makes sure they are good ideas in the first place and then builds on them in a way that cuts through the nonsense you hear about marketing and builds an actionable perspective that just has the ring of truth about it."
—DAVID C. BAKER, ReCourses, Inc
Nationally recognized speaker
at *HOW Magazine* Design Conferences

"If there were a business school course on brand building, Allan would be its professor, and this book would be the text."
—BRYAN MATTIMORE, President, The Growth Engine Co.
Author: *99% Inspiration: Tips, Tales and Techniques for Liberating Your Business Creativity*

Briefs for Building Better Brands
Tips, Parables and Insights for Market Leaders

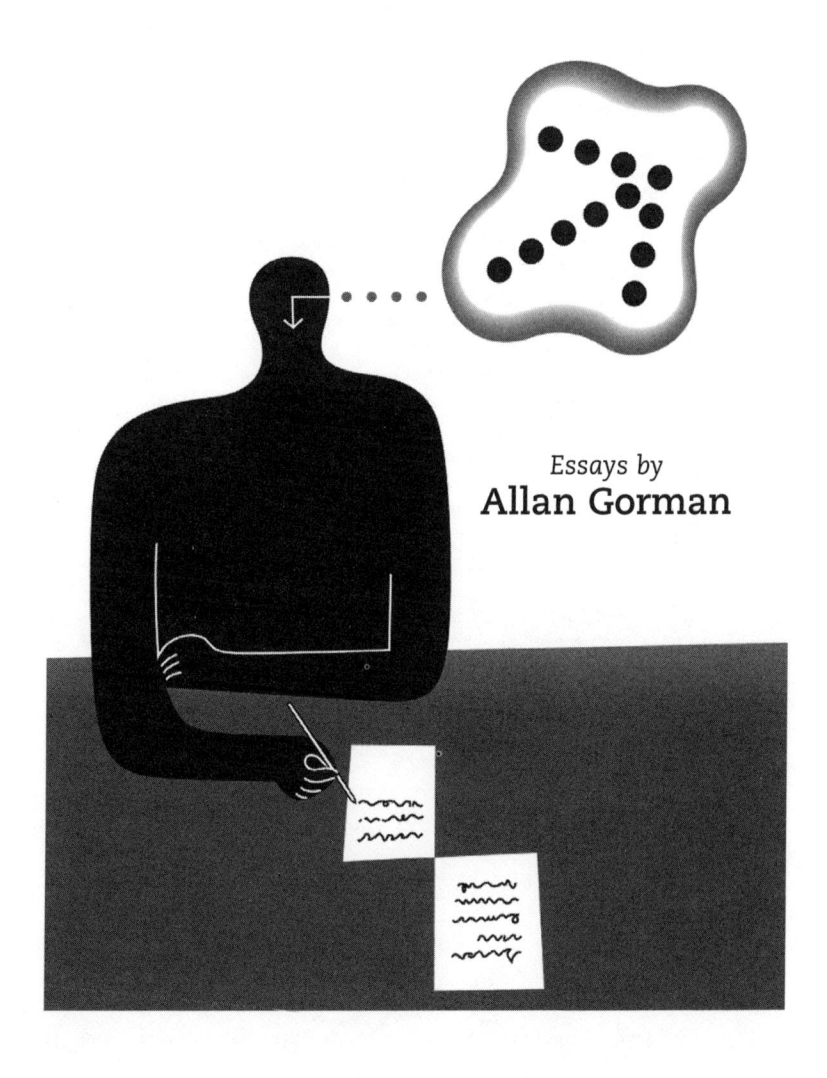

Essays by
Allan Gorman

The publication is designed to provide competent and reliable information regarding the subject covered. However, it is sold with the understanding that the author and publisher are not engaged in rendering legal, financial or other professional advice. Laws and practices often vary from state to state and if legal or other expert assistance is required, the services of a professional practitioner should be sought. The author and publisher specifically disclaim any liability that is incurred from the use or application of the contents herein.

George Silverman's 28 Secrets of Word-of-Mouth Marketing (on pages 100-113) are adapted from the book: *The Secrets of Word-of-Mouth Marketing: How to Trigger Exponential Sales Through Runaway Word of Mouth* by George Silverman, Published in New York, NY by AMACOM Books, ©2001. Used with permission.

Copyright © 2004 by Allan Gorman. All rights reserved.

An AGCD Brandspa™ Book
215 Glenridge Avenue, Montclair, NJ 07042

www.brandspa-llc.com

Printed in the United States of America.
First Printing: June 2004. All rights reserved.

Publishers Cataloging-in-Publication
(Provided by Quality Books, Inc.)

Gorman, Allan
  Briefs for building better brands : tips, parables and insights for market leaders : essays / by Allan Gorman.
   p. cm.
   Includes index.
   LCCN 2004090305
   ISBN 0-9749169-0-0

   1. Brand name products--Marketing.   I. Title.

HD69.B7G67 2004   658.8'27
                                   QBI04-200090

This book is printed on acid-free paper. Text set in Caecillia and designed by the author.

*Dedicated to my mom, who had the gift
and my dad, who had the gab.*

*And to Susan and Sam, who'd clobber me
if I didn't put their names in the book.*

Acknowledgements

Whenever I glance at this page in other books, the author leads with how much work is involved – and how many people are involved – in actually getting a book published. Like them, I've found that writing is the easy part. The rest is "roll-up-your-sleeves", "one-foot-in-front-of-the-other" hard work that's just impossible to do alone. And so, my deepest gratitude to all those who've been so supportive and helpful making the book that you're holding a reality.

I'd like to thank Robert Middleton, my friend, coach and mentor who got me started on the path to writing business papers and sharing my knowledge. My gratitude to former client and current friend Tom Jones, who originally had the idea to bundle my stories into a book. To my friend and assistant Bebe Landis, and wife Susan and son Sam, who have to listen to all these stories over and over; and have to suffer my insecurities on a daily basis. Thanks for putting up with me.

My gratitude to the many clients who've put their trust in me, stretch me, let me hone my craft, and teach me so much about how to communicate more effectively: Kevin Gallagher, Glenn Newman, Joe Pavlichko, Jerry Burke, Barbara Woldin, Denise Gabrielle, Bob Strub and others come and gone at Croda Inc; Lorraine Terraneo, Stuart Goldstein, MaryBeth Zeman, et. al. at

William Paterson University; Bill Dauster and Norma Abreu of Jersey City Medical Center; Barbara Pidgeon at Roche Pharmaceuticals; Doug Fenichel at K. Hovnanian Companies; Tom Eastwick and Martin Klangasky of Eastwick Colleges; Allan Feldman, Phil Raia, Tim Orenbach and all the players at LMCA; Faith Rice, Judit Ungar and Mark Levine at the Tourette Syndrome Association; to name but a few.

Thanks to the teachers, mentors and brilliant advertising and marketing minds who've contributed to what I know—especially those I've had the good fortune to meet and work beside at: the School of Visual Arts; NYU; Dodge & Delano; Grey; FCB; Y&R; The Marschalk Company; Martin Landey, Arlow; and many other great institutions and communications firms.

I've learned so much from the professional and business alliances I've made in groups like: The Art Directors Club of New Jersey; The New Jersey Ad Club; Business Marketing Association; American Marketing Association; Commerce and Industry Association; and Ironbound Businessmen's Association. Thanks for the support of my friends at the Gateway Two Toastmaster's Group; and also the dynamic and exciting people I've met through the Tri-State Chapter of the National Speaker's Association.

Heartfelt thanks to my good buddy Ted Polmar of Design Graphics for our breakfast meetings and his trusted advice. To always smiling Richard Magid, John Federico, and my supportive new peer community at the Lets Talk Business Network. And thanks to John Howlett for his helpful ear and advice.

Also to all the peers, fans and allies who took the time to look over my pre-release copy and bestow their kind comments on my work: Jay Conrad Levinson, Al Ries, Jeffery Fox, Bryan Mattimore, Don Gabor, Mike Sisti, Gayle Turner, David Baker, Liz Lynch, Linda Rooney, Dennis Peters, Karen Post, Gary Watson and Eliot Phillips.

To Doug Ross for the book cover art and "thinking" man icon—it captures the imagination and knowledge in all of us —great job!

I'd like to acknowledge and recommend Dan Poynter and his comprehensive and inspiring *Self Publishing Manual* and www.parapublishing.com for its insightful, up-to-the-minute and helpful advice. And thanks to Ellen Reid of Ellen Reid's Book Shepherding for her hand holding and expert guidance.

There must be hundreds of others whose names I've overlooked who've influenced me and are equally responsible for the creation of my writings as anyone I've mentioned. You are in my heart and I extend my gratitude to all of you too.

Finally, thanks to all the readers of the "Briefs for Building Better Brands" monthly newsletter, and to all of you who've purchased and shared this book.

My commitment is to being a welcome presence and serving you.

You inspire me to keep on learning and improving, and I promise to keep on sharing what I hope you find useful.

—AG

Contents

                                                                            Page

Acknowledgements 11

Preface 17

1. Do you know why you're in business? 19

2. How to get your brand inside that exclusive club available only to the market leaders..................24

3. What's the price you pay for putting off your marketing? 32

4. The consequences of board think 38

5. Not as advertised (What happens when a brand doesn't meet the customer's expectations) 43

6. Branding lessons from the Orp man 47

7. It's all about becoming THAT! 51

8. Finding a great meme can turn your product or service into a charismatic brand 58

9. Let's have some serious fun (When employees love the brand, customers love it too) 61

10. Should you fire your ad agency and hire a PR firm instead?...66

11. Just look at all those Santas! (The dangers of dressing up in someone else's costume) 72

12. Aren't you a slave to good design? 76

13. "Why you? What's in it for me?"
    (Offering them a solution-based answer) 80

14. The entire State of Texas sabotaged by a few nuts!............ 85

15. Vision and values for market leadership 89

16. Your visual message:
    Is it hurting or helping your sale? 92

17. Branding: The emotional shortcut to winning
    the rational sales argument 96

18. Brenda, Bob, and Bill: A lesson in the power
    of brand experience 100

Appendix A: Special Reports

BONUS 1: George Silverman's 28 Secrets
of word-of-mouth marketing 108

BONUS 2: AGCD's Brand IQ Test 121

Appendix B: Resources

Recommended Reads 130

Helpful Web Sites 134

Contact Information 140

Index 144

Product Order Form 152

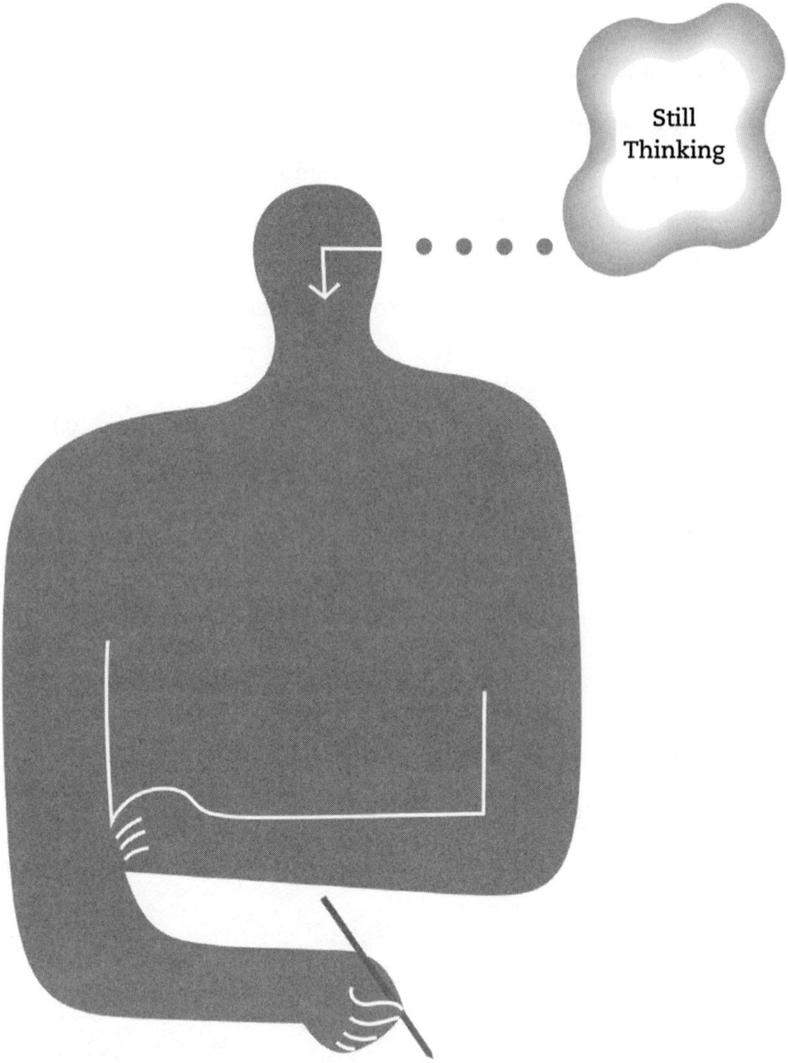
Still
Thinking

Preface

I'd given my talk entitled "Ten Marketing Secrets for Building a Sexier Brand" to Professor Sandy Becker's Marketing MBA candidates at Rutgers a few times in the past. But the other night he asked for something a bit different.

"These are Gen-Y and Gen-Xers," explained Becker. "They've been immersed in the fundamentals of marketing for the past four or five years, are very sharp and sophisticated, and are about ready to test their wings. Do you think this time you could pose them with a bit of a challenge? Get them to think about what they would do to tackle a particularly fickle brand problem. Something they can sink their teeth into and relate to. Give them some real-world examples."

(My inner knee-jerk reaction to this was "Well, I'm not Weiden & Kennedy. I don't have Nike or Target as an account. Why not call them?" But I kept those thoughts to myself and instead tried to offer a good solution.)

"I've got an idea," I shared. "Why not let them work on my company? We're a small creative boutique that, a few years ago, was feeling the effects and pressures of a dwindling market. We went through a one-hundred-eighty-degree brand overhaul ourselves." (That's how come I know so much about this stuff.) "How about if I come by and share some of the problems we faced with your class? I'll share our business and marketing history up to the point that we realized our messages just weren't working anymore. Then I'll ask them what they'd do to help. I'll act like their client. How'd that be?"

Professor Becker loved it and so did the class. Because, after letting them guess at some tactical fixes for a while, I revealed the steps that we actually followed and are still following to transform ourselves from a "just another commodity vendor" into something truly different and unique: a company offering a delightful brand experience that's redefining expectations.

In these stories I'll share some of what we're learning on our journey.

Do you know why you're in business?

Ask most executives about what the objective of their business is, and they'll probably tell you that it's primarily "to make as much profit as possible."

But they'd be wrong.

Of course, it's crucial to make a profit—you can't have a viable business for very long unless you do. And, because your spread sheet is easily the most measurable way to track your brand's viability, it's simple to understand why "profits" can become management's focus and business definition.

But to view the purpose of your business strictly in terms of the bottom line is a limiting perspective that often makes for ugly and irresponsible business and marketing practices that can actually hurt profitability—or even kill off your brand in the long run.

The big problem with the "maximize profitability" mindset is that it forces focus towards a traditional "buy low/ sell high" marketing strategy and mentality...

> *What can we do to trim expenses?*
>
> *What incentives do we use to get more people to buy our products?*

But this isn't a marketing strategy or marketing mentality at all—it's all about selling; and unfortunately, selling is antithetical to building successful and profitable brands.

Change your objective from creating more profits to creating more customers.

Perhaps if we'd consider that the real purpose of your business (or any business, for that matter) isn't just "to make a profit" but is actually "to create customers," it would force us to view things a bit differently.

Then the focus shifts away from just selling and truly towards marketing.

A different idea entirely.

Selling is all about getting past the objections, closing the deal, moving on and doing it again—lots of times to make lots of sales. "Buy low/sell high," and make as much as you can as quickly as possible—with little or no regard to customer satisfaction. The focus is on you and what goes into your pocket.

Marketing, on the other hand, is all about delivering satisfaction, making friends, and developing long-term relationships. And the interesting thing is, that this selfless strategy can actually turn out to be more profitable in the long run.

Shift your business mindset to creating customers and you begin to understand that what's important isn't all about what you make, what you do, how you do it, or the deal you offer.

Rather, it's all about the customer... what he needs and how you can satisfy his needs. How the product you make or service you provide adds value and delight to the customer's life.

"What's in it for them?" instead of "What's in it for you?"

When a company can change its focus to creating customers, it leads to new thinking, innovation, greater employee satisfaction, and a sense of service that transcends the confines of the company's present structure. It also makes business fun.

All companies say they want "out of the box" thinking.

To get it, they need to shift their focus to customer-centric ideas instead of profit-driven ones.

Brands aren't created by the company; they're created by the public.

I recently participated in an America Marketing Association forum on branding. One of the participants suggested that a successful brand could be defined as "the delight one feels from the experience he or she had with the product or service."

Many companies still have the mind that a brand is something that they can make: that how they package it and promote it is responsible for its success in the marketplace.

While it's true that packaging and promotion can often contribute to a brand's favorable perception, the actual "brand" is made in the public's mind... and is a result of the subsequent story that the audience creates and spreads.

A brand's story is never solely based on the brand's features and benefits and systems, but rather on the delight (or disappointment) that your publics feel as a result of the experience they had. They may cite some of the features as justifications; but what makes the brand—and what actually will turn them into customers (and ambassadors who will spread the good word)—is solely the delight.

I was recently delighted by a brand that demonstrated these principles.

My wife and I just got back from a cruise to Alaska aboard the Celebrity *Mercury*.

Celebrity is consistently rated tops among the "Best Cruise Ships in the World" in *Conde Nast Traveler* polls. It's ranked as a five-star company—certainly not because they're bottom-line focused.

Do you think if they followed a policy of cutting costs, skimping on quality, and cutting discount deals they could ever earn such a reputation? No, the reason for Celebrity's "celebrity" (I couldn't resist the pun) is because their corporate focus is not solely based on maximizing profits, but rather on creating happy and loyal customers.

They've studied customers' desires and tailored their products to satisfy (or more than satisfy) those desires. They've defined the Celebrity Experience as "a true departure" and carefully handpick and train all their employees to understand that—at bottom line—their job is to help every passenger on a Celebrity ship "depart" from their normal lives into a world of comfort, pampering, luxury, and "delight."

They did that for me and now I'm a raving fan—a real "customer"—who'd definitely use their services again, and certainly wouldn't mind if they made a profit—because I feel confident that they will then turn those profits back into a delightful experience that I'll value.

Understand that the purpose of your business is creating customers by adding value and creating delight, and you might soon start to realize "celebrity" with your audience too.

How to get your brand inside that exclusive club available only to the market leaders

I n the town of Montclair, New Jersey, where I live and work, we have a trendy and exclusive nightclub called *Diva*. It resembles something you might find across the river in the Big Apple and, just like they do over there in Manhattan, every Friday and Saturday night, a bunch of hopefuls line up outside behind a velvet rope, waiting for their chance for acceptance. Some of the crowd—regulars and a few who look especially attractive—get to cut the line and are ushered right in to the inner circle, while others often wait for hours—or just don't get in at all.

It kind of resembles what happens when we try to get new customers, doesn't it? Some of our competitors—regulars and a few who look especially attractive—get to cut the line and go right in, while some of us wait for what seems like years for just an appointment—or just don't get in at all.

So what's the secret of getting into the club? Why do they only pick the regulars and those who look especially attractive? Even more importantly, how do you become one of them?

The answer lies in finding a way to gain acceptance into your prospect's own hip and exclusive establishment called the "Inner Circle of Choices Club."

The Inner Circle of Choices is a private and exclusive club that each and every one of us has, and is unique to our own values, tastes, and preferences. Think of it as an imaginary hangout for representatives from all of the choices in your personal and private world. Included are your choices for friends, where and how you choose to live, what you choose to wear, which team you choose to root for, and—as it relates to brands—which ones you choose to buy and where you choose to buy them. Products and services that are included in your personal inner circle are intimate friends with bonds that keep you loyal to them. Like your family, these are not just casual relationships but trusted allies that play a pivotal role in your support system.

Your goal for growing your brand is to have it become a valuable and welcomed regular guest at your prospect's circle of choices club. But there are a few things you need to understand about his club before you can even come close to realizing this goal...

a. The Inner Circle of Choices Club is the basis for all repeat business.

Think about your own inner circle. Isn't it true that there are products, services, and brands that you always choose over and over again? Oh sure, on occasion you might be seduced into straying and trying something new, but you always come back, because the things in your circle are special to you.

b. Admission to the club is by invitation only.

Within the circle are only those items that we choose to have there—we decide who gets in and who doesn't. The relationships we have with those in our club are only with things we feel attracted to. Speaking of attraction, here's an important lesson to remember, and remember well...

> *Attraction happens when we become attractive,*
> *and never happens when we come on too strong!*

c. You are not in the prospect's club, and your competitors are.

It's a tough pill to swallow, but realize that this is why so many of the marketing and selling messages we're exposed to every day are completely ignored. You have to appreciate the futility of saying (through marketing and advertising messages): "Don't buy that product or service that's in your inner circle, a trusted member of your club that you value and know so well. Buy from me instead, a total stranger that you're suspicious of and know very little about!"

d. At least five bouncers are standing in your way.

Just like at Diva, a bunch of tough-looking goons keep guard outside to block your entry into your prospect's club. These very specific areas of resistance—key characteristics of the human psyche—need to be addressed and overcome if you are to gain any access at all. But if by some technique (and of course there are techniques) you can neutralize these gatekeeper's powers, it is quite possible to get inside and enjoy all the riches that abound. We have identified five key areas to focus on that are so fundamental that they can be regarded as universal—crossing all cultures, age groups, religions, and social classes. Overcoming these barriers is crucial for your brand's success...

Bouncer #1. Identity. To make sense of our world and decide how to relate to it, people need to classify and pigeonhole people, things, places, etc. If you're to gain access, you must convey meaning for your product or service that is beyond that of simply an industry participant.

Bouncer #2. Emotion. Probably the most important thing in a person's life at any given moment is the way he feels. To get in his club, you need to find a way to connect with him on an emotional level.

Bouncer #3. Self-Interest. The primary motivator of human activity is self-interest. Find a way to tell the prospect how his self-interest will best be served by letting you into the Inner Circle, possibly at the expense of one of his oldest friends.

Bouncer #4. Recall. People's short-term memory is extremely volatile and evaporates quickly. You must provide a good way to help people remember and recall your brand when they're ready to make a purchasing decision.

Bouncer #5. Resentment. People have an underlying resentment towards salesmanship, marketing, and advertising and see it as an intrusion on their privacy. You need to find a way to overcome this resentment and connect with people in a way they find both appealing and engaging.

> It's just that…
>> you need to connect in order to succeed…
>>> but the customer doesn't want to know
>>>> about you, and has already tuned you out…
>>> and entry into his club is by invitation only…

> *and you can't force your way in the door…*
> *and he has his goons trained to stop all*
>   *of your sales efforts…*
> *and you need to get inside because that's*
>   *where the profits are…*
> *and you need those profits to grow*
>   *as a brand, etc., etc.…*

Ok, Ok, Ok! There's a way to get into the Club.

(Why would I write this if there weren't?) But it requires that you must do certain things in a certain way, every single time. In other words—you'll need a good system.

So here's an abridged version outlining the basics of the system we employ…

1. Develop a clear identity. Employ good market research to find out just what your identity is in the eyes of your best customers. What's the value of your service or product—not from your perspective, but from theirs? Use what you learn to distinguish yourself from your competition in a meaningful way. Your brand's identity must be built on a platform that sets you apart from everyone else (on purpose!). The prospect is going to pigeonhole you. Just how would you like him to do it?

2. Offer a benefit. What's in it for him to let you in his club? Your product or service is going to solve a problem (perhaps one he doesn't even know he has) and he's going to enjoy the results. Your premise must be built on a great benefit that the prospect can easily understand and relate to.

3. Appeal to his emotions. How do you want the prospect to feel after listening to what you have to say? Align your creative marketing techniques with your desired emotional response.

4. Help him recall your name. Employ a unique device to help him recall who you are when he's ready to purchase what you're offering. A unique graphic, a turn of phrase, a combination of the two—just make sure it's meaningful and identifiable with your company and reminds him of the benefits you have to offer.

5. Penetrate his "noise" barrier. Find out how to penetrate his resentment and resistance to sales. He's developed a "noise" barrier to filter out all but what's pertinent to his life and values. You are an annoyance and he will tune you out unless you're offering some interesting information that he can use.

6. Be all that you say you are. Make sure that the claims you make and the promises you offer are supportable and sustainable over time. Don't make claims that are unsupportable or change your products and services to support them.

The secret to making all of this work lies in your ability to take all this criteria and to distill it down to a brilliant essence that comes across as being very simple and clear, but still neutralizes the imposing barriers standing in your way to admission to the club. The answer may not come too easily, but with a good system in place, the answer will come; and more and more customers will extend the invitation for you to join them in their Inner Circle of Choices Club—a very great honor indeed.

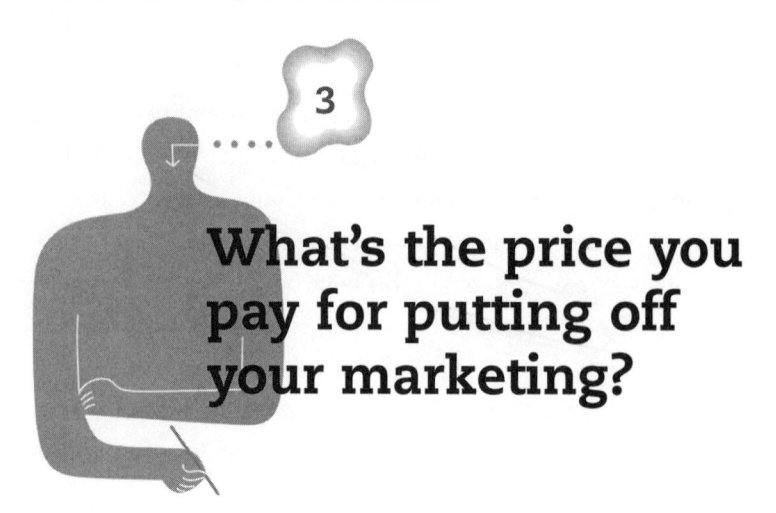

What's the price you pay for putting off your marketing?

I keep procrastinating.

Even though I'm very proud of these marketing briefs, I will confess that sometimes it can be a chore sitting down to write them.

I keep finding excuses and other things to do instead of prospecting and cultivating the lifeblood of my business. Me, who professes to be somewhat of a scholar and teacher on marketing issues, would sometimes rather do just about anything else.

So what's the price you pay for putting off your marketing?

Most of us are the same when it comes to promoting and selling our products and services.

Since the rewards of our efforts are seldom instantaneous... hard to make direct correlations to...and almost impossible to control, it's hard to get excited about putting in a lot of time writing letters...calling up strangers who don't want to speak with you...and spending a ton of money on "fluff."

At least when you sweep up a dirty floor, you can see the "before" and "after" results right then and there. But marketing?

It's quite rare, especially in a service business like mine, for a potential prospect to hear your story once and say, "Sure. I need what you're selling right now. Come right on over so I can give you some money!"

Market now, so that when he is ready to give away his money, you're the one he'll want to give it to.

In the past two decades, the word "branding" has become all the rage.

Why?

Because smart people charged with marketing have come to realize the power of a familiar identity to sell lots of product—and also command premium prices.

But what's branding?

Simply, it involves making yourself so desired in the mind of a prospect that he wouldn't even think about considering an alternative when the time comes to take advantage of what you're selling.

Branding takes bragging.

Let's just suppose that you and your competitor offer exactly the same product—same price, same quality, same service, same everything. The only difference between you and him is that he constantly brags about himself and you don't.

If and when a potential prospect is in the market for that product, who's gonna get the business? Probably not you.

Now, you and I both know that your product is much better than his, right?

Trouble is, the world out there doesn't. They only know what he keeps telling them—and that's the only story they remember.

Branding takes being unique.

So how do you shut that loudmouth up? By talking louder?

Well, you could try talking louder; but this tactic just makes you a "me too," and confuses the issue with your prospects.

By saying the same exact thing, you might hurt your competitor's sales; but in the long run, it's probably not going to help yours much either...

"I'm the best in the business!"

"No he's not, I am!"

"No he isn't, I am!"

After a while, customers don't know that they can believe either of you; and, since you guys are spending so much time trying to outshout each other, they're probably inclined not to listen to either of your stories.

No, the trick to becoming a real "brand" is finding your very own story to brag about.

The idea is to become unique and attractive in your own right—to invent and own a distinct category in the prospect's mind so that he wouldn't even think about another alternative.

Branding takes action.

Branding happens by becoming famous. It comes from finding a unique, more attractive position and then promoting it—over and over and over—in as many ways as you can—until they start to "get it."

(These days, some experts claim that it will take at least six exposures for any given message to even start to become identifiable—and if you then stop promoting, just an instant to forget it.)

Marketing to become branded takes a lot of effort...It can be hard to justify with tangible evidence...And it isn't inexpensive. (Small wonder most of us keep avoiding it.)

But if you don't start taking action now...to find something great to brag about...to package it in a unique and attractive way...and to get the word out on the street so that you can bury your competitor, you can bet that your competitor will take the opportunity to do just that to you.

Here goes my shot...

IF YOU WON'T STAND FOR REMAINING PARITY, AND WANT TO DISTINGUISH YOURSELF AND ATTRACT BETTER CUSTOMERS, YOU NEED TO READ MY BRIEFS FOR BUILDING BETTER BRANDS.

I'VE CREATED A BRAND NEW CATEGORY OF PROFESSIONAL CALLED THE "MARKET LEADERSHIP ADVISOR".

A MARKET LEADERSHIP ADVISOR FOCUSES ON HELPING YOU IMPROVE BOTH YOUR INTERNAL AND EXTERNAL PERCEPTIONS SO YOU CAN DIFFERENTIATE YOUR BUSINESS WITH A DISCERNABLE VALUE THAT YOUR AUDIENCES WILL SPARK TO.

OVER THE YEARS, MY ADVICE HAS HELPED CUSTOMERS REALIZE MILLIONS OF DOLLARS IN INCREASED SALES AND BECOME STANDARDS OF EXCELLENCE IN THEIR INDUSTRIES.

WHEN YOU'RE READY TO DISTINGUISH YOURSELF AND "REALIZE MARKET LEADERSHIP," CALL ME! ETC... .

(In all caps and bold... so you'll notice and remember!)

Now, what are you waiting for? Get out there and start bragging!

The consequences of board think

A few months ago I went to a strategic planning session for an organization I belong to. Of course, as it is with most organizations (or businesses), the main concern on the agenda was membership (or how to get more customers). This wasn't the first session they've had, mind you. Planning (and planning and planning) is something they've been doing on a regular basis for years. That's what boards do. What took place at this meeting was a review of what the organization had accomplished toward their goals since the last planning meeting. This was followed by a discussion of whether the plan should be changed... whether the whole organization should be changed... whether the audience should be changed... and lots of new suggestions about more changes they could implement to get new members.

There was a lot of good stuff, and I'm sure that some of it will even get acted upon.

And then, no doubt, they'll have another one of these meetings in a short while to analyze what they did and then make even more plans and throw out even more good suggestions to make even more committees and even more activities.

Something "big" is missing from this picture.

See, while everyone at the meeting thought that his or her ideas were really swell—and for sure, some of them really were—continuing to add and change physical features and benefits is not going to fix the real problem.

The real problem is that they just don't have their brand's core marketing message right. And until they get it right, the concern over membership (or your company's concern about new customers) is going to continue be a pesky issue that lingers, festers, and frustrates.

Market leadership is achieved through owning an identity as the "one and only" in your category. It's the result of occupying a specific piece of positively charged emotional real estate in your prospect's mind that no one else can lay claim to.

You do this by making sure that your core value proposition (CVP) is clear, attractive, meaningful, and fulfills a need. Then you find a great way to articulate this CVP in an emotionally compelling and easy-to-recall way. You create a "viral" marketing message that keeps going...and going...and going...(just like the little pink Energizer Bunny), so that the message becomes reinforced each and every time your audience hears or sees your good name.

Then, all the activities and ideas you create make more sense, because they're all done in support of the articulated "big" idea.

The big idea needs to be bigger than the organization.

Most companies struggling with their marketing often create their messages hit or miss. Oh, for sure, there have been plenty of great and memorable copy lines and logos created over the years; but in most cases they've been arrived at through trial, error, and intuition. And, because they were just "made up," these messages have often become vulnerable to change with each new regime making new plans and implementing new ideas.

This is a dangerous scenario. Changing your message once your identity is established just confuses and frustrates the audience. A new core message (unless it's a quantum leap better than the current one) can kill off all the positive equity you've already built into your brand name. Worse, it can also kill off your brand.

All the more reason to not "shoot from the hip," but to take the time to understand exactly what your message should be...to make sure it's right...and that it will be a promise you can live with and deliver on for a long, long, long, long time.

Use a foolproof approach to finding out the real "core" message.

There's a logical and surefire way to developing exactly the right message that will make your customers respond and swear their loyalty to you.

Ask them what they want!

Ask your organization and its members and its prospects what makes them loyal. Ask people who reject you why they are not loyal and what makes them loyal to someone else. Ask as many sources as you possibly can. Then gather up and analyze all their responses to find what the real reasons are—the ones that lie deep below the surface—the emotional "whys." Then go back and ask them which of these emotional "whys" is the most appealing. Their answers might surprise you.

At our firm, we guide clients through a unique, structured process of discovery, refinement, and testing to ultimately find out the true "why" that will make an audience accept your idea.

The process takes an investment of time, hard work, and money, but it always works to get the message right. And it's been used to build some of the world's leading brands.

Take the time to find out the real emotional "why" before attempting any more "fixes" to your brand. Then you'll be on your way to crafting an image that will be a magnet for new customers—not because of a new feature or marketing idea somebody on the board thought up—but because your audiences are crystal clear on what you stand for... and the real reasons to join your club.

5

Not as advertised
(What happens when a brand doesn't meet the customer's expectations?)

A few months ago, a brand-new, architecturally striking, and very inviting-looking animal hospital opened not too far from our home.

Since the vet we had been using for the past fifteen years is overworked and extremely busy—sometimes you have to wait an hour or more—my wife and I agreed that we might try this cool-looking new place the next time we had a need.

Our dog Ziggy is getting up in years and my wife brought him by for a check-up.

The building was well equipped and looked as great inside as it did from the facade—it even won an architectural award. But the young doctor she saw didn't seem to know what he was talking about and didn't make much of an impression. There was another vet involved with the practice and maybe he was different.

(STRIKE ONE!)

Ziggy gave us all a bit of a scare recently—he fell down our front steps and wouldn't put down his back paw. He was clearly in distress.

I called the new hospital to see if the doctor could see him. The receptionist offered to schedule an appointment for the next day. "Unacceptable. This dog is in pain—it's an emergency! Can't something be done to squeeze him in?"

Her response was that there would be extra charges and that she'd have the doctor call me back.

(STRIKE TWO!)

A half-hour later, the doctor called. He listened to my description of Ziggy's symptoms and agreed that he should come in right way. At this point I registered an objection to extra charges since Ziggy was a registered patient of the hospital's. (Mind you, they never said how much these extra charges would be.) The doctor's response was that since my request is an inconvenience—they'd have to shift around schedules, extra paperwork, etc.—they need to add extra charges to offset their time and troubles.

I asked him how much the charges would be and he said: "Ten dollars."

Did they really have to make a big issue about extra charges for a lousy ten bucks? Why not just train the receptionist to say, "I'll see if we could squeeze you in, but there's an extra ten-dollar charge for emergencies." Or why not just add it to the bill as a line item? Who'd question it?

(STRIKE THREE!)

Now for the appointment.

Now I'm not feeling so good about being here at this fancy place. It's the other doctor this time. My wife didn't get such a great feeling about the other guy, and I don't feel so hot about this one either. His manner is cold. He examines the dog in silence and before sharing any diagnosis or educated guess with me, says, "I think we'll need to do some radiographs to see if there is any damage to the bone. If you'll excuse me for a moment, I'll be back with an estimate. It's our policy to get half our fees in advance before treating the animal." He walks out the door and leaves me in the examination room to sit and wonder how astronomical the fee is going to be.

(STRIKE FOUR, FIVE, SIX—A THOUSAND! YOU GUYS ARE OUT!)

What do you make of this scenario? Are these guys interested in treating sick animals and providing service to customers who are troubled about their pets, or are they more interested in how are they going to pay off the mortgage on their beautiful new building?

And by the way, the only customers in the building when I was there were Ziggy and me. (Thanks for squeezing me in and sorry for the big inconvenience, Doc. I'm sure it won't happen again.)

Moral:
Fail to deliver on your customer's expectations and you soon won't have any customers.

Turned out that Ziggy had just shocked a nerve—he's doing just fine now, but we're going back to our old vet next time.

Branding lessons from the Orp man

Some of us in the office were having a conversation about the effectiveness of brand distinction the other day, and it reminded me of a cute little episode I thought I'd share with you.

A number of years ago, my wife and I were on a NYC subway train going across the Manhattan Bridge into Brooklyn.

Standing at the end of our car was a young man in his twenties dressed in a metallic gold spandex jumpsuit, wearing a necklace with one of those flashing red and green light thingies dangling from it. His face was painted gold as was his hair, and he was carrying a beat-up tenor saxophone.

He wasn't terribly clean and he was carrying a cup. Everyone in the car knew that we were about to be hit up for a handout.

Sure enough, as the train began creeping across the bridge, in a clear commanding voice he said...

"Greetings, earthlings!... I am from the planet Orp.

Unfortunately, my spaceship has crash-landed and is in the repair shop.

It needs a very expensive part and I must have the funds to fix it so I can get back home.

On Orp, we communicate like this..."

He then played a one-minute, wild and absolutely ridiculous Jazz riff on his tenor.

He continued...

"Could you please help me with a very generous donation so that I can fix my spaceship and get back to where I came from? I am very anxious to get back home, and quite frankly, the food on your planet stinks!"

A man got up from his seat and went to the end door to get into the next car to avoid having to cough up, but the door was locked. Orp man turned and looked at him and said:

"There is no escape."

I felt so entertained by his novelty, his sense of humor, and his non-menacing approach to what was no more than begging that I did indeed feel compelled to give generously. (I feel guilty for saying this, but I normally give street beggars a fairly wide berth—I generally find them scary, upsetting, and an annoyance.)

This fellow really got to me and won me over; and even though it's more than twenty-five years later, I wouldn't mind paying a little extra to see his act again.

Orp man really understood marketing and the power of branding:

He studied and understood his audience.

He took pains to ensure that his product was distinct from his competitions'.

He packaged and positioned himself uniquely, and virtually re-defined pan-handling to be the only one of his kind.

He knew his brand mission, which wasn't just to get prospects to spend money, but to make it a truly unique begging experience; and this was supported by everything he did.

His presentation was built around an indelible mind trigger that would create positive awareness and irrational loyalty for years and years to come.

He delivered value that far exceeded customer expectations.

He won you over emotionally, and in turn, commanded a higher price.

His brand was so unusual and created such a buzz, that plenty of nonpaid brand ambassadors (like me) still feel loyal and are willing to give him plenty of free advertising.

Wouldn't it be great to have as much success from your brand-building efforts as the man from Orp?

7
It's all about becoming THAT!

Recently, I had the honor of being interviewed by entrepreneurial business mentor and marketing guru, Robert Middleton (www.actionplan.com). We talked about why positioning your product or service properly is so crucial to the survival of your business.

Robert's own positioning, or value articulation, is *helping independent professionals who are struggling to get more clients*; and he chose to have me as part of his Marketing Mastery Series (workshops, tapes, manuals, etc.) because of my expertise and experience working on Madison Avenue with larger brands.

Do some of what the "big boys" do apply to the little guys as well?

Do they apply???!! Well, absolutely!

Marketing—the lifeblood of your business—is of critical importance, and the principles are basically the same whether you're a billion-dollar multinational or one guy or gal working out of the basement.

There's some confusion about what a brand is.

Robert and I started our talk with our definition of a brand.

Often, business people think that their brand is their company or product's name, a logo, a tag line, or (if they've worked on it) what they say in their "elevator" speech.

They think that these things need to be clever or attractive to make their brand stand out. Then they try to imitate the way they do it at the big agencies on Madison Avenue.

So first off, let's be clear that great logos, tag lines, names, etc.—while very important—are nothing more than brand articulations.

The brand itself is ever so much more; and to start your marketing efforts without first fully understanding this will almost always hinder your chances for success.

Your brand is your story.

My definition of a brand is: *The story that people will tell when asked to recommend your product or service to someone else.*

In other words, you do not make the brand at all. Your brand is actually created by the public—by their perceptions, thoughts, and experiences—by how they define you.

Making your brand successful (or the art of branding) is, to a large extent, the result of helping the public understand just how to tell the correct story for you.

A strong brand is the result of delight.

A strong brand happens because its story is remarkable. The perception and experiences people have are delightful, fun, and pleasurable to recall.

In other words, the strength of your brand correlates to how the qualities you have—either real or imagined—are of value to your customer.

A strong brand isn't because of a cool logo, or that it has a particularly catchy tag line. It is because the experience of the product or service, or the individual representing it, was something over and above just what the recipient expected. It is an experience she wouldn't mind having again, and wouldn't mind sharing with others.

It takes a scientific method to understand just what your customers think is delightful.

Professionals in every business do their homework. They study the lay of the land. They are up on what their competition is doing. They gather as much knowledge as possible before applying their craft.

You should do the same before attempting to build your message.

Although much of marketing is art—and, admittedly, done better by some than others—incorporating some science into your efforts will ensure that you're not just shooting from the hip with ideas that you or your agency think are cool and nifty.

Research will guarantee that you're actually providing a promise of value that is relevant and desired.

I'd put my money on a blandly presented, but meaningful brand story, derived from research, over a beautifully executed, yet irrelevant message, every time.

Ask the public for help in crafting your brand's story.

Here are some of the steps we follow with our own clients before creating anything...

a. An internal audit of people in the company to get a clear idea as to how they think they'd like their brand to be perceived.

b. Interviews with their customers, prospects, former customers, distributors, and even never-to-be customers, to get an idea of what they think the client's brand is all about. We'll also ask these audiences what an ideal brand might be like.

c. Based on what we learn, we then go back and help our clients brainstorm a number of potential "appeals" that their audiences might best connect to (and that the company can realistically deliver on).

d. We market-test these appeals until we discover just what "story" makes the most sense to tip the scales in our client's favor.

We now know that our message makes sense—not because of what we think is clever— but because the public told us: "Yes, I would consider your brand a better choice because you give me...**THAT!**"

What I've outlined might seem like a lot of fancy market research reserved for sophisticated marketers—and it is! (Hey, that's why they're sophisticated.)

But that doesn't mean that a one-man operation can't also employ the same methods. They can just be done on a smaller scale and more anecdotally than through expensive surveys and focus groups.

Promise THAT! And make the way you deliver it your bond and your brand.

We've started to understand just what the public thinks actually does—or would—make you special, that they'd choose you because you can give them... THAT!

So, THAT! should become the platform for your entire business.

THAT! is your promise and you may even want to change the way you run your business to make sure that you will always fulfill THAT! promise for them.

Further, you should make it your business to over-exceed at fulfilling THAT! promise, doing what you do better than anyone else can.

Here's the real secret!...

> *It's really the excellence and service you'll deliver when fulfilling your customer's expectations that's going to create the delight that will give them something to talk about.*

Commit to THAT! story.
And tell it in every way you can.

Now you understand why positioning is so important. It helps the public remember your story. In fact, it is your story.

And now you can work on the elevator speech. Now you can get the agency to make cool logos, unique tag lines, great product names to help you articulate you're unique because you can deliver... THAT!

Incorporate the same core message—"We deliver THAT!"—into your ads, the way you answer the phone, your sales pitches, and proposals. Put THAT! into all of your communications.

THAT! will be what you stand for and how you'll be remembered, and THAT! is what will make you the strongest brand.

Finding a great *meme* can turn your product or service into a charismatic brand

What the heck is a meme? In his book *Rapid Response Advertising*, Geoff Ayling attributes the term to an evolutionary biologist named Richard Dawkins who coined the word to represent a self-replicating idea that changes perceptions. In his context, memes are responsible for the changes in civilization by permanently altering the way people view things. Fire was a great meme. So were the wheel and the invention of written language.

In a brand-building context, memes are powerful pieces of communication—either verbal or visual (or both)—that have such power as to alter people's perceptions of your product or service.

Think about these advertising themes and symbols...

Just Do It!

Think Different.

The cranky insurance company duck.

Have it your way.

The Pink Bunny with the drum.

The little talking Chihuahua.

If asked, you could probably name dozens of others.

These are examples of strong and powerful memes. You know exactly who they stand for, and what the brands that own them stand for too. And every time you see the image or hear the line, it self-replicates and reinforces the perception of the brand that owns it. Great memes can help build brands that define their categories.

You might now say, "Well I have a tag line or I have a logo. Why don't I have a charismatic brand?"

And here's the twenty-dollar answer… It's not just the meme that's important; it's also what the meme communicates.

What all great brand-building memes have in common is the emotional component that answers every consumer's magic question: "What's in it for me?" See, what makes it memorable isn't really the symbol or the words—it's the benefit. A good meme repeats the benefit over and over every time you see it or hear it.

Answer your customer's "What's in it for me?" question simply, with a bit of poetry and a benefit that means something, and you'll be on your way to a great meme—and a charismatic brand that can define its category.

9
Let's have some serious fun
(When employees love the brand, customers love it too)

I'm at my local Volkswagen dealership and the founder's son is walking around with his Mom handing out Christmas bonus checks.

I've seen this fellow before and he impresses me as taciturn and uncomfortable. He's in his late 30s-early 40s and looks and acts like a bean counter—stiff, protective and defensive. It seems a strain for him to part with the envelopes—not a pleasure and an expression of gratitude, but an annoying obligation.

"Ok. Here's your bonus check. Thanks for a good year. No, don't shake my hand. I don't want to take a chance of getting grease on my starched white shirt. Ok, let's go back to work now."

I get the feeling that, although the employees are receiving a gift, most will be unhappy with this bonus check (no matter what the dollar amount), and would jump at the chance of working somewhere else.

Witnessing this scenario doesn't make me feel that I'd want to work for this owner either. And, as a customer, it makes me rethink my commitment to his dealership. If this guy doesn't value his employees, does he value his customers? Does he think that we're an obligation too?

The experience your customer has is a reflection of how your employee feels.

With all the pressures that fall on business owners and managers, many of us overlook the importance of maintaining a happy and inviting corporate culture.

We think that our employees automatically owe us the courtesy of being nice and accommodating to our customers.

But we all should take a break once in a while to remember that the happiness of our employees is often the result of how good they feel about the company they're working for.

The same "out-of-the-box" thinking that goes into creating a winning brand through a unique customer experience needs to transform your internal culture as well.

Serious fun from the top down.

I was listening to a recent interview with Matt Weinstein who wrote the book *Work Like Your Dog—50 ways to Work Less, Play More and Earn More*.

Matt's book outlines a bunch of scenarios for bringing fun and play into the workplace that, beyond just the event itself, can have a positive effect on your employees throughout the year.

A unique and unexpected fun experience—just once in a while—can have a contagious and residual effect that will leave your company smiling all year long.

Fun that gets talked about beyond the event.

Fun in the workplace alleviates stress in the office. It boosts morale, creates loyalty and pays off in monetary dividends that result from happy, enthusiastic workers.

Here's how it works...

- Someone brings in a bouquet of flowers and gives it to a co-worker to watch over for just an hour. That person then has to pass the bouquet to someone else in the office. The anticipation of who's going to become chosen next becomes a great game that can keep everyone smiling and can last a few days—and get talked about for months!

- You take your employees on a buying trip to the mall. You give each a hundred bucks and one hour. The caveat is to buy at least three things for themselves with the money. If they fail to get three (or more) items, or if they don't spend the money on something personal, they forfeit the hundred bucks. If they don't spend all the money, they have to return the balance.

  Watch how your employees leap to life and buzz about how much fun it was. Watch them show off and compare the purchases they made. Watch how they smile like kids in a candy store. Doesn't this beat a cold, obligatory bonus envelope at Christmas time? (Of course, the dollar amount can be $200 or $500, or even more; and the venue can change too. And why wait for Christmas? Sometime totally unexpected is even better!)

- Instead of a casual Friday, have a formal Friday—where everyone has to dress up in formal evening wear. A twist on this is dress the supervisor day: let all the charges in each department decide what each supervisor has to wear next Friday (within reason of course). Then have a fashion show of the supervisors and award a prize to the department with the best outfit.

- Have some internal classes run by your local history museum, zoo or astronomical observatory. Hire a fortune-teller for a day.

These are a few examples, but you should look to create a few unique fun-builders of your own—that stem from the manager's heart, but take expression on your employees' faces.

Fun has a serious effect on your bottom line too.

Imagine walking into a firm where everyone has a big grin on their face. You might start to smile too. There's something contagious in the atmosphere.

Now imagine one where everyone is stressed and wearing a frown. The service is rude and you feel like you are burdening them.

Who'd you rather do business with?

Which firm would you want to go back to?

10

Should you fire your ad agency and hire a PR firm instead?

In their latest book, *The Fall of Advertising and The Rise of PR*, father and daughter marketing gurus Al and Laura Ries try to build an argument that advertising as a brand-building tool has outlived its effectiveness.

Their perspective is that clever ads—and many of the ads done today are extremely clever—are merely created as art for art's sake. That the ad agencies creating them have become blinded to the task of effectively promoting client's products and services, and have become consumed with impressing themselves and their peers with witty, award-winning creations. Also, that the more creative and startling the ads are, the less effective they become.

They indict the ad community for losing sight of its purpose and suggest that the billions of dollars marketers spend annually on paid media are no longer worth the investment.

Instead, Mr. and Ms. Ries try to make the case for good public relations, and that the "buzz" created by third-party endorsements is the primary tool we should be using to build today's winning brands.

Advertising vs. PR is the wrong argument.

I think there's a missing piece in their logic. The argument shouldn't be about which marketing tool to use (and that's what ads and PR campaigns are—tools).

In reality, there are still plenty of effective ads done; and public relations is for certain an important and effective way to impress customers, too. Both are important to your marketing, and each should be considered by how effective it will be at any given time.

But if you're a marketer truly concerned about the success of your product or service, deciding whether to fire your ad agency and hire a great PR practitioner instead is probably not your first—or best—solution.

What's of primary importance is to look internally first.

The real issue is whether or not your audience sparks to your product's or service's value proposition.

At base, what makes an advertisement work (or not), or what makes a good PR campaign successful (or not) is whether (or not) the audience perceives genuine distinction and real value from your offering.

Both paid advertisements and free press coverage are great ways to tell your brand's story—provided there's a good brand story to tell.

It's the brand story that's key to building loyalty, sales, and success.

Earlier today, I passed a highway billboard with a chair hanging off its side.

The face of the board was painted to resemble an IKEA product hang tag showing a price of twenty-nine dollars.

To my mind, this is a great advertisement. If I saw a news story that said: "IKEA sells chairs for $29," it probably wouldn't have stuck with me, made me smile, or compelled me to go to IKEA as effectively as the ad does. (So much for the Ries' theory.)

But really, what makes this ad work so well, isn't so much its award-caliber creative. What makes this ad click is that it successfully tells a unique IKEA brand story that people can care about and can relate to.

On the other hand, Starbucks got a lot of PR "buzz" and was built into a mega-brand without the use of a giant ad budget. But not because its PR firm came up with a strategy that was particularly brilliant. It's because the Starbucks concept and follow-through is so wonderful. Its brand story is one that people can care about and can relate to.

We recently had a meeting with a religious institution looking for help. After doing a little research, we came to the conclusion that what was at issue wasn't so much a marketing communications campaign, but that the brand itself has outlived its relevance.

We could create great and clever ads and milk the media for lots of press exposure, but since relevance is the issue, would we really fix the problem?

They need to find or create a new and fresh brand story that people will care about and can relate to.

Compelling ads and great press can create curiosity and get you a look, but if what your audience sees isn't appealing, neither your advertising nor your public relations efforts will work very well.

But if your brand story is great—one that people care about and can relate to—won't it automatically get the "buzz," and won't your paid messages be so much more effective?

If the news isn't good, don't kill the messenger.

The best marketing people—advertising and PR professionals—are great storytellers. When they create fiction from their heads—as entertaining as it might be—it's just an empty suit.

But when there's something substantial to say—when there's true distinction and appeal—both advertising and PR team up to become powerful allies in building your brand's success.

Before any marketing, you and your agency (or agencies) should work together to...

> *Do some research to understand your audience(s) better. Find out what they need, how they perceive you versus the ideal, and what you need to do to more closely resemble their ideal.*

> *Find ways to distinguish your brand better and deliver your promise in a unique, memorable and compelling fashion.*

> *Develop a distinct brand story that people will care about and can relate to.*

> *Help you and your entire organization take pride in knowing that your product or service is superior to every other alternative and develop new ways to more consistently deliver your brand's promises above and beyond just what's expected.*

Determine the right mixes of marketing mediums that make the most sense for an effective return on your investment.

Remember that the tools you use to tell your story are effective only to the extent that you have an effective story to tell.

11

Just look at all those Santas!
(The dangers of dressing up in someone else's costume)

In earlier chapters of *Briefs for Building Better Brands*, I've touched on the importance of having an original identity that's distinguishable from everyone else's. We've discussed why bragging about the same thing and looking the same as the market leader won't help your sales all that much, and will probably just make you look like an also-ran.

Now that the holiday season is on us, we can see this phenomenon in vivid action.

You know who Santa is, right? He's real easy to spot. Look for a jolly, slightly rotund, elderly gentleman with a white beard who wears a fur-trimmed red suit, wide black belt and black, stacked-heel boots. (Well, at least that's what the ad industry convinced us Santa looks like—the real Father Christmas bore little resemblance to this modern fellow, who was drawn by Haddon Sundblom in 1931 as an advertisement for the Coca-Cola Company.)

Just look at all those Santas!

This month, there will be literally thousands of guys—standing out in the street, in stores, on TV, in ads and billboards, wearing costumes—fur-trimmed red suits with black belts and boots. They're all going to try and convince you that they're Santa; and that if you were smart, you'd buy what they were hawking.

But you and I both know that all these guys aren't Santas at all. They're just a bunch of fakes. I'll bet even all those little kids who have to sit on the old man's lap for a holiday photo know that guy's not for real. He's just another grandpa in a rented costume.

Imitation Santas are so prevalent, that if the real St. Nick ever did show up, he'd probably have to submit to a DNA test to prove his legitimacy (and by the time the lab results came back, there would be a bunch of fake St. Patricks running around town).

How does this make the real Santa feel?

Now, is Santa upset that there are a bunch of wannabes out there trying to pass themselves off as him? Is he concerned that imitators are trying to steal his customers and erode his market share?

Of course not. He's Santa Claus—the market leader and the real brand name—the real deal.

The real Santa's laughing all the way to the North Pole Commercial Bank. And the reason he's so jolly is that all those fakes are great advertising for him! Their presence is just reinforcing his preferred brand name, building more customer loyalty, increasing his market share, and, as a bonus, making him lots and lots and lots of holiday cash.

Every time you see a fake Santa, it's a free ad for the real guy.

A few marketing lessons from Mr. Claus.

So are there some lessons here?

Well, of course there's the obvious lesson that imitation only helps the imitated.

Next, the more you are recognized as a market leader, the better the chances you'll be imitated. But this should not be a worry—imitation is great, free advertising that will only reinforce your stature and brand name.

There's also the not-so-obvious lesson embodied in true leadership—and the real Santa Claus: that what builds your following, makes you attractive, loved, and desirable to the masses is not a result of what you're trying to get from them (which is usually the imitator's focus). It's really the honest value you purposely try to give. Your generosity is what customers will perceive as attractive and what will make your brand the one that's preferred.

And isn't that what service is all about? Giving?

Aren't you a slave to good design?

Admit it. Aren't you a slave to good design?

Don't well-designed materials—brilliantly conceived, exquisitely printed, well crafted, beautifully fabricated— draw you in, just like a moth is drawn to a flame?

Don't you want to have them... and make them an extension of yourself (and a reflection of your great taste)?

On the other hand, don't things that are poorly crafted, poorly designed, just plug ugly—leave you cold and indifferent—and make you want to walk the other away?

You're a slave to good design.
So what does good design have to do with marketing your brand? Well... everything.

Each of us has his own personal club that I like to call "the inner circle of choices" club. Into this club are allowed only those that we find attractive and appealing. Things that don't measure up to our standards and criteria just don't get in.

Doesn't it stand to reason then that, since your visual appearance is the first piece of information a stranger receives, the more attractive you are, the better your chances of getting into his club? And becoming his preferred choice for the type of product or service you're offering if and when he needs it?

If you have high aesthetic standards, doesn't it make sense that your customer does as well?

With this argument, there should be no skimping or cutting corners on a great presentation.

A computer program won't give you good design.
With the advent of personal computers and software that have made it "so easy even you can do it" (or so they lead you to believe), there's been an undermining of the design profession by unskilled novices who can now use a computer program to make things look "good enough."

The software companies have played a dirty trick on us.

Using "templates" and the tutorials they provide can, admittedly, help people whose calling isn't necessarily design, create materials that will look better than what they could make without these sophisticated computer tools.

But this isn't good design.

Good design, in the hands of a skilled and experienced pro—who eats, sleeps, and breathes aesthetics—is a unique nonverbal solution to a communications problem.

And you just can't get a unique solution using tools and templates made for mass consumption.

"Good enough" isn't good enough to help you become a market leader.

The old adage is true—first impressions are lasting impressions.

And the first impression you make can actually make or break your business.

The quality of your materials—the way they're conceived, designed and printed—from your logo and business card to your Web site, to the office décor, even to the way you dress—is the first, and one of the most powerful experiences a customer will have of you and will forever dictate the ideas he will have of your brand.

Do you want that experience to be that you'll settle for "good enough"; or do you want to be perceived and remembered as the one who's unique, distinctive, and the very best choice in your category?

There's no substitute for professionalism in good design.

Hire the very best professional to get the very best design you can.

Look for a communications solutions provider who will help you establish a unique visual "voice" that reflects the quality, personality, and vision of your brand.

Don't cheap out—spend what it takes. It's an investment in the future that can pay off in dividends a novice and a software template will never be able to provide.

"Good design" is a unique, nonverbal solution to the communications problem of conveying that you're the best there is.

Be happy that you're a slave to good design… because your customers are too.

13

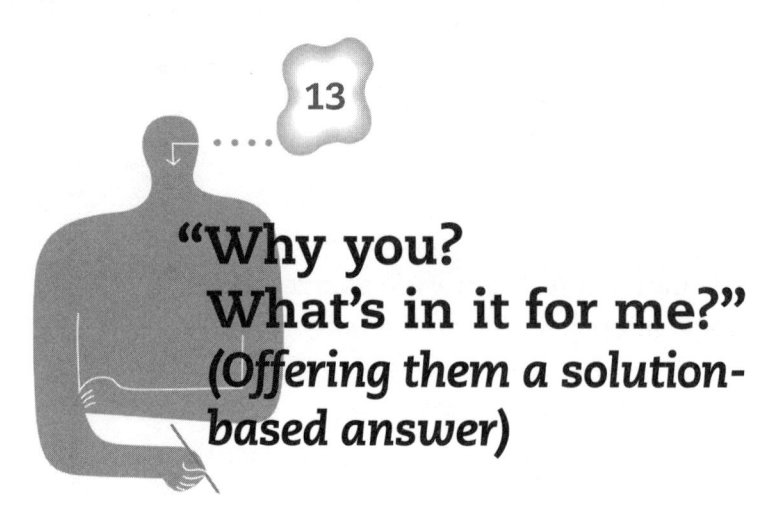

"Why you? What's in it for me?"
(Offering them a solution-based answer)

I got a call—someone got my name out of the Yellow Pages. He asked if I did graphic design and then asked: "How much do you charge for a brochure?"

Now it's perfectly understandable why he would approach me this way—he doesn't know me, doesn't know my company, doesn't know our work, and has nothing to base his decision on other than price.

In other words, to him I was just a graphic designer—a commodity service.

So my reply was, "Well, it depends on the brochure. But tell me first, what do you want to do with this brochure? Why do you want it? Who will receive it? And what do you want them to do as a result of receiving it?"

We then entered into a ten-minute discussion where I was able—by asking questions and sharing some information —to learn much more about his business and what kind of marketing issues he's facing. Turns out his purpose for the brochure is to introduce his furniture line to retailers (who might not know him).

At issue here, then, isn't really designing a brochure at all—it's helping him develop a good tool to get his furniture line into retail stores.

Now, I don't know enough to advise him wisely yet. But for sure, we will have some more conversations about this; and I promise I'll do my very best to help him achieve his goal.

What I did in this conversation was to drill down to gather enough information so that in the end we might be able to solve his issues with a better solution than just a brochure done as inexpensively as possible (which, in the long run, is much more costly—but that's a topic for another discussion).

Now, in his eyes, I'm not just another graphic designer. I'm a valued marketing communications consultant.

But enough about me, what's in it for you?

Admittedly, so far this little story might seem like a "so what" to you.

But is it? Isn't this story really the basis for all successful sales... and all successful marketing?

It demonstrates that for every successful transaction there needs to be a trading and sharing of enough information to ultimately provide the answer to the buyer's burning question: "Why? Why you? What's in it for me?"

In the story above, I did this by making myself more than just a commodity. Instead I was an interested consultant; and my concern for my potential client and his marketing issues makes my services far more valuable than just "how much?"

And then, should we do business together, my lesson for him will be showing how to get better sell-in by taking into consideration the needs of his client (the retailer). I will help him distinguish himself as more valuable by making sure all his communications efforts answer his buyer's burning question: "Why? Why you? What's in it for me?"

And now you'll always do your best to answer your client's "Why? Why you? What's in it for me?" questions too, won't you?

But enough about you, what's in it for them?

Here's a little something to help you get started on the "solution-based answer" road.

Work on your "audio logo."

This is what you say to someone when asked what you do. Instead of answering "I'm an accountant" or "I have a packaging company" or "We make glass vials," try to create a message that's more solution-based. It should be a simple phrase that identifies your audience and answers the question: "Why? Why you? What's in it for me?"

My own audio logo is usually a variation of:

"I help small- to mid-sized companies who want to crank it up to the next level, find better ways to distinguish themselves." (This is what I told the furniture manufacturer during our chat.)

A good audio logo works better because it hits a nerve.

It helps people identify themselves as a potential customer ("small- to mid-sized companies"); the nature of their problem ("who want to crank it up to the next level") and it offers a compelling solution ("better ways to distinguish themselves").

The closer to home it is for the person hearing it... the more he can identify with it... the more desirable and memorable it makes you. It then distinguishes you in his mind as something other than "just a commodity." It makes you a valuable resource for solving his issues.

Here's a formula you can use to create a good audio logo for yourself.
Try it now... *(You fill in the blanks):*

> "I help _____ *(your target audience)*,
> who want _____ *(address their problem)*,
> get _____ *(your solution).*"

This is a very easy-to-use formula that can work for any service or product, but your audio logo doesn't have to follow it exactly. The part that's important is that it provides the promise of a solution to a problem that they might have. It answers: "Why? Why you? What's in it for me?"

The audio logo does more than just answer their question. It helps you too.

The audio logo is a powerful tool. It works because it clarifies who you help and what problem you can solve for them.

But it does more than that—it clarifies your product or service for you too. Because the audio logo conveys a clear promise, you are now committed to delivering what you say you will—a better solution.

And from that moment on, you won't perceive yourself—or allow yourself to be perceived—as just a commodity ever again. You'll become a valuable ally and solutions provider who can always answer each and every customer's burning question...

"Why? Why you? What's in it for me?"

14

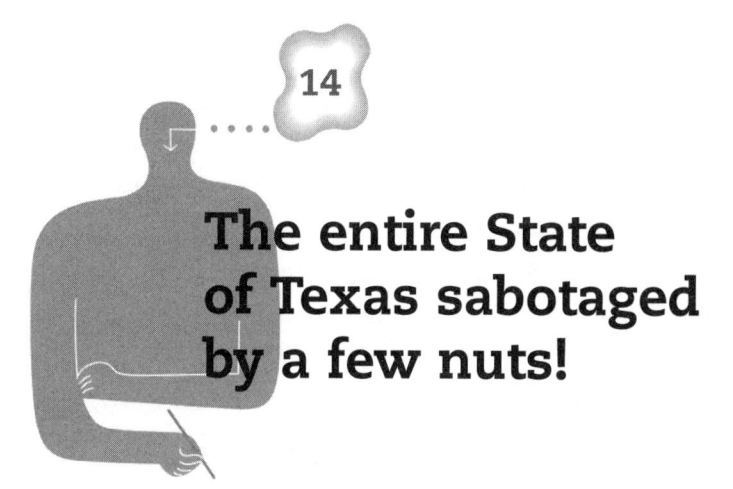

The entire State of Texas sabotaged by a few nuts!

My friend Scott Price, president of NJ Skyline, was strolling the floor at the Fancy Foods Trade Show at the Jacob Javitts Exhibition Center in New York City, sampling the treats offered at some of the booths.

He stopped by the booth for the State of Texas where a young lady was handing out little cups of Texas gourmet cashews.

The warm nuts were scrumptious, so Scott decided to go back for a second helping.

Well apparently, the young lady recognized Scott and made up her mind to send a message to him that she didn't appreciate that he had the audacity to come back for more.

This time, instead of letting Scott have a full helping, she took pains to count out a measly six cashews (about a third of a normal helping), sending a strong psychological message to Scott that he just better not even bother thinking about returning a third time.

And, what's more…

"We just don't extend a warm welcome to no-good, dirty, low-down, rotten, free cashew nut snitchers like you here in the State of Texas! Maybe you should try your luck over in Oklahoma, Louisiana, or Arkansas where they might be a little less vigilant than we are!"

One bad experience—no matter how trivial—can create a bad perception for your brand.

Unwittingly, through her trivial and silly stinginess over a few little kernels (in actuality, she was probably just trying to conserve her cache for other visitors), cashew girl sabotaged the entire State of Texas.

At the trade show, she was a representative for the Lone Star State (or if working for you, would've been an ambassador for your company).

Her insensitivity to her job and actions left Scott with an indelibly bad taste (bad pun!) for Texas. Now, every time Scott sees a cashew, or hears anything about Texas, he's going to recall this episode—and then he'll retell it to others (like me).

For Scott, Texas now represents stinginess. And, by extension—if they could do that to a nice guy like Scott, what would happen to someone like me—who likes his cashews at least as much as Scott does?

I'm for sure going to stay away from Texas!

Your brand is the result of a series of experiences—both good and bad. Maximize the good ones.

But what if the scenario went a little bit differently? What if the young lady from Texas understood that giving out free cashew nuts was a vehicle for spreading good will?

Then, upon seeing Scott for a second time, she might have said (with a smile): "I see you like our cashew nuts. Aren't they delicious? This time I want you to have an extra big portion. 'Cause I want you to remember and tell your friends that's the way we do business down here in Texas... big state... big heart... big portions... big welcome! And next time you have a hankering for cashews, you just think of your friend Helen."

Wouldn't that have been a better story? What good memories would cashew nuts and Texas trigger then?

The desired result of giving out cashews.

Why did her boss ask her to hand out cashew nuts anyway?

Wasn't her job to make Scott want to come back for more? Wasn't her job, giving away free samples of a "Taste of Texas," to build prospect and customer loyalty... good will and "brand fans" who would spread the good word?

Why do you think I write these articles?

Vision and values for market leadership

Certainly creating marketing plans and action plans is an extremely valuable and necessary exercise that needs to be done on a regular basis. But an often overlooked and useful first step in developing a game plan to serve your future marketing efforts is to also write down what you're committed to in some kind of vision and values statement.

This is simply a list of what visions and values you have for your business. The idea is to focus your goals by thinking about, and trying to articulate, why you do what you do and what you want from it.

I revisited my own visions and values for my company and wrote some new ones just this morning. Here they are...

We are committed to being the very best resource for businesses who want to realize more market leadership.

We are committed to the development of innovative and creative strategies, and the creation of superior marketing tools that will help our clients realize better results.

We are committed to learning, and will continually search for useful information, better solutions, and innovative ways to increase the value of the services that we can provide.

We are interested in every client's success and take pride in the contributions we can make to further their goals.

We enjoy finding and realizing workable and sensible solutions that can help others win at what they want to do.

We are committed to finding new opportunities that will require us to perform at the peak of our abilities.

We take pride in the results of our labors on behalf of others.

We will continually renew our commitment to customer satisfaction and quality and will remind ourselves that the services we provide are useful only to the extent that they add value in the eyes of our customers.

We will be a conduit for useful information that can help our clients grow and realize more success.

We like being creative and innovative and can use these God-given talents to help others position, package, present, promote and persuade better.

We are committed to fair, long-lasting, successful, and mutually rewarding relationships.

Now I will take these statements and put them in an obvious place—like tacked up on the walls of our office—to get us back on track every time we lose focus on what we want do, and what we stand for.

Doesn't this sound like a good idea for you too?

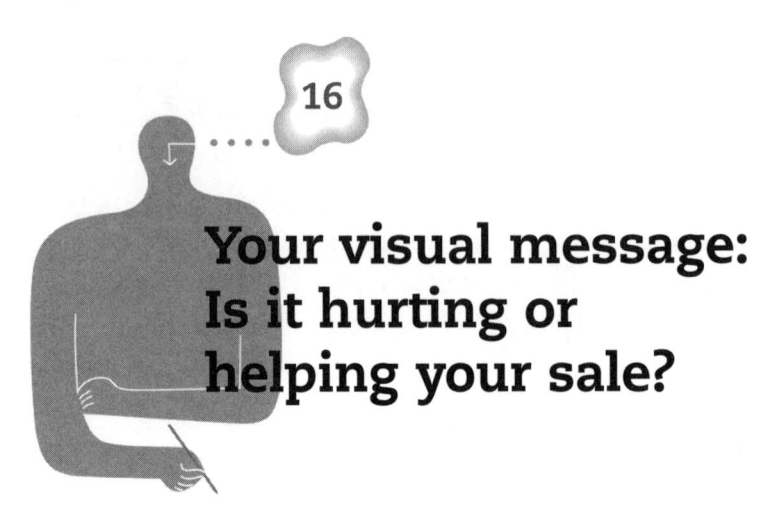

Your visual message: Is it hurting or helping your sale?

Last week I went to visit one of our clients to discuss making some revisions to their company's trade show booth.

We'd designed a "perfect" new corporate identity for this client a couple of years ago and also a corresponding trade show exhibit.

Everyone agreed that it was very striking and interesting, and an exciting extension of their handsome new corporate look.

The trouble is, that in faithfully marrying the booth to their design system, we all lost sight of some critical pieces of information. And this actually hurt their sales.

We neglected to step back and take into consideration their potential customers and what they might be looking for.

That is, while the booth makes this client look important and helps them stand out, it doesn't clearly state what business they're in, show what kind of products they make or convey how they're different.

This will be fixed—and fast.

The meeting taught me a good lesson about the importance of relevance and how it can make (or break) a great visual presentation... and help or hurt a sale.

The story of three storefronts.

Let's take a window-shopping walk down an avenue in a foreign city.

We come upon a striking storefront that makes us stop and look twice.

The architecture and design are of the highest quality, extremely elegant and beautiful—like nothing we've seen.

But the store has a name we can't pronounce or understand.

The window display is very creative and clever, but it doesn't quickly make clear what kind of merchandise they have for sale inside.

What are the chances of us going inside to look around?

Probably not very good.

While the beauty of their presentation makes us say "Wow!" the irrelevance of their presentation makes us say "not for us!"

We come to second store.
This one has a bunch of commodity souvenirs in the window.

The presentation of their wares is nothing fancy, just a lot of stuff with prices all over them.

Will we be compelled to go in? Maybe—if one of the items in the window appeals to us.

But all those price stickers will also make us wary and suspicious. Are they just come-ons? Are they selling quality merchandise? Will they stand by their product if something goes wrong?

It might cause us to think that there are probably a lot of stores selling the same thing; and that, if we do a bit of shopping, we can probably find the item for the same price somewhere else—at a store that feels more reputable.

We walk on.

Now we come to a third store.
This one looks like nothing we've seen before. They have a great name, a great look, and their wares seem like "our kind of stuff"—but with a unique design twist and style.

It looks like it's going to be fun going inside this shop. It promises to be a great shopping experience that won't disappoint.

And it looks like we're going to be rewarded with merchandise, service, and a shopping experience we just can't get anywhere else.

Do we go in? You bet we do!!!

And we'll purposely shop hard for something interesting to buy, too!

Revisit your storefronts.

Your visual presentations are just like these store's window displays.

Unspoken, they need to communicate a unique and relevant message or they will hurt your sales.

Your logo. Your card. Your letterhead. Your ad. Your package. Your office. Your truck. Your Web site. And your trade show booth.

Are they unique and look like nothing we've ever seen?

Do they also say that your wares are "our kind of stuff?" but offered with a unique design twist and style?

Do your visual messages convey that it's going to be fun for a customer to go inside? That he's going to have a great shopping experience and that he won't be disappointed?

Is your design relevant—does it communicate that he's going to be rewarded with merchandise, service, and a shopping experience he just can't get anywhere else?

I use uniqueness and relevance as "gold" standards to measure the power of the brands I work with.

And from now on, I promise that I'm going to use those standards to measure the success of every visual presentation I'm involved with too.

17

Branding: the emotional shortcut to winning the rational sales argument

For the most part, business customers aren't impulse shoppers—they're extremely rational.

Because enormous sums of money are sometimes involved, and their corporate future can often depend on making the right choices, people who buy business products and services will usually follow a deliberate and careful path to a purchase decision.

They'll gather data, peruse literature and Web sites, consult with associates, ask for proposals, and weigh alternatives to make sure that the choice they'll make is correct.

Often, there can be multiple parties involved, keeping each other in balance and making sure that the product or service to be selected will be the very best available to solve the problem at hand.

If customers are going to research choices anyway, does a strong brand really matter?

Today more than ever!

True, in today's information-rich marketplace there are endless resources to find intelligence on just about anything one might want.

But what business buyer really has the time to scour the web and follow every possible lead to look at every possible supplier there is?

In most cases, they'll start with a list of candidates that they already know about and work from there.

This is where branding comes in. You want to make sure your name gets on that list!

Recognizing you as a preferred brand simplifies the buyer's task of assembling his list of viable candidates.

There are more benefits from branding than just making the buyer's candidate list.

For sure, just getting on the list isn't the only benefit to be derived from building a strong brand. As the purchasing process progresses, being a strong brand also gives you a competitive advantage on the emotional side of the buying decision. And make no mistake—the fact that business purchases are carefully considered doesn't mean that they're completely devoid of emotion.

Preference and loyalty plays an important role —just as it does when you buy something for yourself—such as a new car, a vacation, or even a pint of ice cream.

A brand can be a blessing when there's a lot at stake.

There's another emotional element that we should consider also.

People who are charged with making major purchases and, in some cases, selecting mission-critical products and services, have a lot at stake.

The wrong decision can negatively impact their company—in some cases, it can even cost the buyer his or her job!

A strong brand addresses this fear factor. Usually a strong leader has a reputation for quality—that's what makes and helps keep it a leader. But even when there's no apparent practical difference between a top brand and one that's lesser known, the more popular brand will still have a competitive leg up, in that the decision to go with the market leader will always be perceived as the safest choice.

It's also cool to buy the best.

Even in tough economic times, companies that stand for leadership—or those that aspire to it—will look to surround themselves with premium products and services. The quality they buy represents the quality they sell. And leading companies don't compromise, as they've come to realize that saving a few bucks on an inferior product isn't cost-effective in the long run.

Find a way to position yourself as the best, communicate it well and walk a high road. Deliver beyond expectations and become perceived as the market leader.

Become the recognized, emotionally compelling "brand," so that you'll make the list more often and win more of the rational arguments, too.

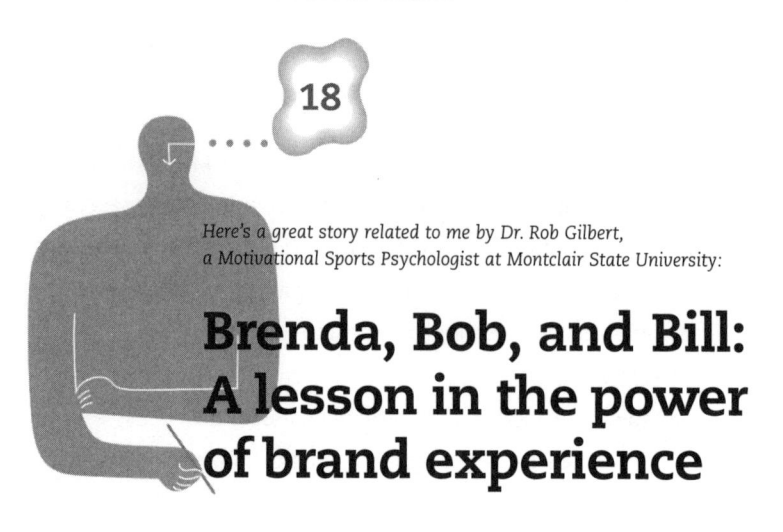

*Here's a great story related to me by Dr. Rob Gilbert,
a Motivational Sports Psychologist at Montclair State University:*

Brenda, Bob, and Bill: A lesson in the power of brand experience

Brenda had a great romantic life with two of the most wonderful guys in the world—Bob and Bill (neither of whom knew about the other).

Each Friday night, Brenda would go on a date with Bob and have a fabulous time. Then, on Saturdays, she'd go out with Bill and have a terrific time, too. All the attention and excitement was fun; and after not so very long, Brenda developed a great fondness for each of them.

Bob was handsome, charming, smart, and witty; Bill was cute, warm, caring, and kind. What more could a girl ask for?

Then, one fateful Friday evening, after a little over a year of dating, Bob decided it was time to move the relationship up to the next level.

Bob pops the big question.

"Brenda," he said, "we have a wonderful time together, and I'd like that to continue forever. There's a great house that I'd love to show you, and I saved the money for a big wedding and a honeymoon you'll never forget. Also, since I was just promoted to sales manager, we'll be able to live quite comfortably. If you'd agree to become my wife, I promise—no, I guarantee—that I'll do everything I can to make you the happiest woman in the world.

"Would you marry me?"

Well this wasn't something that Brenda was pushing for or expecting. And just as soon as Bob popped the question, she instantly thought about her other boyfriend, Bill.

"Well... uh... this sure is a surprise, Bob. I'm speechless. I'm... I'm gonna have to think about it," she replied.

The rest of the evening fizzled. Brenda was distant and lost in her thoughts. ("What do I say to Bob? What do I say to Bill?") Bob was feeling completely ignored, and they even had a little spat. He took Brenda home early and left without even asking for his usual goodnight kiss.

Saturday night, it's Bill's turn.

Saturday night Brenda thought Bill seemed in an especially good mood. He had planned an evening at a hot new restaurant and looked dashing in his brand-new suit. He'd even had the car washed. The meal was unbelievable, and Bill was attentive to her every need. Brenda was having such a wonderful time she'd almost forgotten about the prior evening's unpleasantness.

Over coffee, Bill said he had something serious to discuss.

"Brenda," he said. "I love being with you and I'm honored to be your friend. I love your sense of humor… and I could look at your wonderful smile all day, every day. In fact, if you'd let me do that, I'd feel as if I was just the luckiest man alive.

"Brenda, will you marry me?"

"Oh my god!" thought Brenda, for as soon as Bill popped the question, she thought of Bob. Sure, last night ended on a sour note; but still, her feelings for Bob ran deep.

"I don't know just what to say, Bill. This is all so sudden. I'm… I'm gonna have to think about it."

Bill was hurt and upset. This wasn't the response he was expecting. Then Brenda seemed distant and quiet for the rest of the evening. (Actually, her thoughts had returned: "What do I say to Bill? What do I say to Bob?")

Bill felt ignored and a little wounded. They even had a bit of a spat. Bill took Brenda home, dropped her at the doorstep and left without his usual goodnight kiss.

Brenda's so blue. Can't marry two. What should she do?

Brenda couldn't sleep. Tears welled in her eyes. In just two days, she'd gone from two wonderful suitors—to maybe none.

As she prayed and prayed for the right answer, who should show up to save the day, but her dear old fairy godmother? (Who else?)

"What seems to be the problem, dear?" she squeaked.

"Oh fairy godmother. I'm so blue. Bob and Bill have both asked for my hand in marriage. I love them both and just don't know which of them to say yes to. Can you help me decide?"

"Of course I can! That's exactly what fairy godmothers are for."

Here's what her fairy godmother told her to do:

"Get out a big legal pad and a pencil and draw a vertical line down the middle of the page.

"On the left side, write down everything you like about being with Bob, and on the right side everything you like about being with Bill.

"Then cross out all the similarities and things that aren't that important until you're left with just the differences.

"I have to go out shopping for a nice dress to wear to the wedding and will be back in a few hours. By then you should have your answer."

Brenda weighs her choices.

"It's worth a try," Brenda thought to herself. And so, she got out a legal pad and did exactly what the fairy godmother suggested.

Boy, did Bob ever have a long list… and so did Bill.

It wasn't such an easy exercise. But finally, by the time her godmother returned, she had made her decision.

"So how'd you make out?" asked fairy godmother.

"The choice was obvious all along," said Brenda. "I'm going to marry Bill, of course!"

"Why? What was the difference?"

"Simple," Brenda replied. "See, when I'm with Bob, he makes me feel like I'm with the greatest person in the whole wide world. But when I'm with Bill, he makes me feel like he's with the greatest person in the whole wide world.

"And that's a feeling I would like to live with happily ever after."

The key to winning your customer's hand lies is providing a great brand experience.

Let's analyze some of the story to see what made the difference.

As marital material, Bob seemed to have some great things going for him. He was handsome, charming, smart and witty. He offered lots of "value-added" features (like a new house, a trip, and material comforts), and was willing to promise— even guarantee—that he'd do everything to make Brenda happy.

Bob's "sales pitch" was designed to point out his value and distinction over other would-be suitors. (Sounds a lot like what many advertisers try to do, doesn't it?)

Now let's look at Bill's approach. He set his mind to showing Brenda a good time (not out of character for him). Bill was attentive and doting. His proposal didn't focus so much on the hard features and benefits he could deliver, but rather on the continuance of their great experiences together. Bill didn't try to hard-sell, as his focus was, and always will be on "Isn't Brenda's happiness a joy to behold," instead of "Brenda'd have to be a fool to consider someone else."

I'd pick Bill too. Wouldn't you?

Appendix A

Some enlightening and useful reports

Bonus #1:

George Silverman's twenty-eight secrets of word-of-mouth marketing

Edited by Allan Gorman

In his wonderful book, *The Secrets of Word-of-Mouth Marketing*, George Silverman provides a thorough and useful lesson on how to use and harness this incredibly powerful marketing tool.

More than one thousand times more effective than paid advertisements, promotions, direct marketing pieces, and even one-to-one individual sales meetings, word of mouth can, by far, be the most important medium in any marketer's toolbox.

Recently, some smart marketers have begun to realize that getting people to talk often, favorably, to the right people in the right way about your product or service is far and away the most important thing that you can do as a marketer.

George's book goes into great detail about why word of mouth works so effectively and many ways to generate it for different types of businesses and products and in different situations.

But for a quick and practical guide to creating your own word of mouth plans, I've outlined twenty-eight of the secrets (actually there are many more than twenty-eight) George thinks are important to consider and remember.

Secret #1 – Selling is mostly illusion. Ads, brochures and direct mail rarely sell products directly. They almost always work through an intermediate mechanism, such as a third-party influence, or word of mouth.

Word of mouth multiplies the effects of advertising and salespeople.

Never take an ad or send a mailing or call on a customer without first thinking about the word of mouth implications, particularly about how the activity can start or intensify the word of mouth chain.

Evaluate every element of a marketing campaign by its potential to cause a positive word-of-mouth chain reaction.

Realize that conventional marketing, at best, can only get people interested in your product, but it's word of mouth that triggers their purchase. And, that if they're already interested, spending more money on conventional marketing is mostly a waste. Instead, spend your money on triggering more word of mouth.

Secret #2 – By influencing word of mouth directly, sales can be increased three to ten times or more! Shoot for big increases with a word-of-mouth campaign. A traditional ad campaign—even if it's a smashing success—can usually increase sales by 10 to 20 percent at most. Instead, shoot for a 100 percent increase by actively incorporating word-of-mouth strategies. This way, even if you "fail" by only achieving half your goal, you will still be a hero.

Secret #3 – Word of mouth is the best way to speed the decision-making process. Pre-digest the buyer's decision to purchase your product by showing how someone else made that decision. Instead of viewing word of mouth as a way of getting someone to look at your product, look at it as a way to speed their purchase decision.

Secret #4 – Word of mouth is as easy to structure as traditional advertising. Map out your word-of-mouth plan with the same rigor you plan your advertising, sales campaign, and other aspects of your marketing.

Develop a strategy that includes: the problem your word-of-mouth campaign is trying to overcome; who the audience is (both demographically and psychographically); what you want them to convey about your product and to whom; why your product delivers in an extraordinary way.

Secret #5 – Word of mouth can be a thousand times more powerful than conventional marketing. People only act on a tiny handful of the thousands of ads and sales calls they receive each week. But they act on many, if not most, of the recommendations they get from friends and advisors.

Treat your word of mouth with the respect—even awe—that it deserves. Your product's reputation is what sells it—not what you say about it—but what they do.

Secret #6 – Word of mouth is the most neglected force in marketing. Realize that when you neglect something powerful you are in danger, but when you tame something this powerful you're at a distinct advantage.

Secret #7 – It is almost impossible for your product to succeed unless it has massive word of mouth. Research the word of mouth that is going on at various levels of your marketing. Know what people are asking each other and what they're answering.

Do everything that's legal and morally possible to stimulate massive word of mouth. This is your first priority as a marketer. Everything else is small potatoes.

Secret #8 – Word of mouth either explodes at an exponential rate or it fizzles. Don't do things halfway. Plan out your campaign and then implement all you can as fast as you can.

Word of mouth is a critical mass phenomenon—like nuclear fission. If you're going to launch a word-of-mouth campaign, don't be wimpy about it. Do a blitz. Go for broke.

Secret #9 – There are lots of reasons why word of mouth is so powerful. All of these, once understood, can be used to your advantage. Become a student of why word of mouth works. Don't assume that it works just because it's unbiased. That's just the tip of the iceberg.

Secret #10 – Word of mouth's most significant characteristic is its ability to deliver experience. The time it takes to gather direct experience before, during and after trial is what often restricts a product's growth. Hearing about other people's experiences makes prospects more comfortable and more willing to take the leap from interest to desire.

Secret #11 – There are many different kinds of word of mouth, all potentially controllable. Word of mouth isn't just customers talking to other prospects. It can be what experts say; word of mouth among salespeople and dealers; word of mouth among employees; traditional press PR; implied word of mouth; endorsements and testimonials; and so much more. As many word of mouth channels as possible should be taken into account in any campaign.

Secret #12 – Different types of decision makers need to hear different types of word of mouth at each stage of the buying cycle. There is a different type of word of mouth appropriate to each kind of customer. For instance, an innovator won't want to hear that your product is "tried and true." On the other hand, the majority won't be impressed with how "innovative" it is. Each type of adopter needs to hear a different kind of word of mouth from experts and peers at each different stage of the "decision to buy" process.

Try to identify the correct wording for the word of mouth that will be successful for each type of customer, particularly what language will get them past the bottlenecks.

Secret #13 – The sequence of your word of mouth is just as important—and sometimes more important—than the content. Don't just try to get positive word of mouth. Be precise about the right messages, timings, sequence, and sources of your word of mouth. Without all four working in your favor, your word-of-mouth campaign will fizzle.

Secret #14 – Consider two levels of word of mouth: expert endorsements and peer-to-peer word of mouth. Each is more powerful than the other at different stages of your campaign. It only takes a pebble to start an avalanche. One expert endorsement, delivered at the right time, in the right way, from the right person, can result in more sales than your entire sales force can deliver in a whole year. Use experts to talk about the upside "potential" of a product.

Conversely, experts can't convey the experience of the product in the hands of the average user. Use peer-to-peer testimonials to show how it works in the hands of the "average Jane or Joe."

Secret #15 – Confirmation and verification are more important than information. Don't rely on word of mouth to present the best picture of the product. That will be the job of conventional ads, brochures, advocacy media, and sales people. Instead, word of mouth can confirm and verify the information. As in Secret #14 above, people first want information to know what the upside is ("What's in it for me?"). Then, if the product shows promise and they are convinced that the product will make a valuable difference in their lives, they will seek out claims verification and confirmation that the product will work out in a situation similar to their own. This is why employers often ask for recommendations and check references.

These confirmations and verifications are almost always sought through word of mouth.

Secret #16 – Word of mouth is the navigation of expert influencers. Realize that "experts" aren't a homogeneous group. They come from varying spheres of influence—on a local, regional, national, and sometimes international level. Often there will be a "trickle-down" effect, with the national and international experts influencing those at the regional or local level, who might confirm each other's opinions as they talk with each other. This will result in more widely held beliefs.

Secret #17 – Experts are more approachable than ordinary people—but only through total honesty. Experts are more approachable than you think. But you must be honest and you must have a superior product and you must not waste their time.

Experts are always looking for new tools to recommend and, even though you may think that you have a great product, will only respond if they think you have a tool that will solve the problems of their constituency (their sphere of influence). They will recommend things that make them look good and further reinforces people's image of them as experts. And that's what makes them want to get behind your products.

Never try to manipulate experts. They can see it coming miles away. Be open and straight with them. They know where you're coming from and always want the best products to succeed.

Secret #18 – When it comes to experts, credibility is more important than fame. Don't confuse expertise with fame. Many info-gurus might not be all that well known except in their particular field. What makes them recognized and followed are their vast knowledge, extraordinary thinking ability, and proven expertise in applying that knowledge to practical real-world applications. Being recognized as an expert also makes them respected for their honesty and unbiased opinions. They will just as quickly share a negative about your product as they will a positive. If the positives far outweigh the negatives, they will become great supporters.

Choose them for their knowledge and credibility and not for their fame. (Of course, if they have both, so much the better—they'll have a larger sphere of influence.)

Experts can be your strongest allies, worst enemies, or totally indifferent. How you go about finding them can influence each.

Secret #19 – There are many reliable mechanisms for delivering word of mouth. Don't wait for good word of mouth as the result of a clever ad campaign or promo. Use as many channels for delivering your message to experts and peer-to-peer ambassadors as you can. Workshops, seminars, videotapes, co-ventures, endorsements, referrals, networking, public relations, the internet, studies, and many other means can be effective tools for reaching the right parties. Each delivery channel has its own special set of rules and should be studied for its effectiveness and efficiency.

Secret #20 – Word of mouth should be approached systematically—as a campaign. Map out, budget, coordinate, integrate, and systematize your word-of-mouth efforts. Uncontrolled and isolated word-of-mouth events often have no effect.

Secret #21 – Word of mouth among your sales force can be more important than word of mouth among your customers. If your salesmen aren't sold, how can you expect your customers to be?

Don't think that a rah-rah sales meeting will do the trick. Your sales force, just like other customers, need to see the product accepted by people outside the company before they start to get fired up. The one thing that overrides everything else is independent proof that the product is superior.

Secret #22 – Research the naturally occurring word of mouth so you can know what your customers are actually saying, what prospects ask, and whether your customers' answers are persuasive. Don't run conventional focus groups, or surveys, in which people are asked, "How would you describe this product or service?" Be unconventional, by customizing groups and surveys to hear exactly what prospects ask and what your customers' actual word of mouth sounds like.

Secret #23 – Experiment with different persuasion articulations to see which ones can influence natural word of mouth. Add to your focus groups and surveys elements of persuasion. Then you can actually hear what changes people's minds.

Secret #24 – "Canned" word of mouth can be almost as effective as powerful, spontaneous word of mouth. Use video clips, audiotapes, the Internet, transcripts of interviews or magazine reprints to deliver word of mouth when you can't deliver it live. It may seem hokey to you, but this is precisely what your customers want in order to make their decision.

Secret #25 – In word of mouth, unlike conventional marketing, negatives can be more reassuring than positives about your product. Don't be afraid of letting a few negatives slip into your word-of-mouth communications. In fact, if they are completely missing, the omission may be glaring and destroy the credibility of whatever material you're presenting. A few negative remarks keep your product from appearing "too good to be true." Just be sure that you've quickly addressed and put into place a good system for addressing the negatives.

Keep in mind that people actually want to try your product and want it to work. But they need reassurance that you have a system in place for handling the negatives.

A discussion of the negatives can, paradoxically to conventional marketing, offer more credibility for your product and actually help your sales.

Secret #26 – Word-of-mouth "advertising" is a contradiction in terms. Advertising is advocacy by the company and rarely presents a fair picture of the product. People are skeptical about advertiser's claims and boasts. They've experienced too much false puffery and tend not to believe advertising. Word of mouth, on the other hand, is seen as unbiased and truthful—the exact opposite of advertising. Don't confuse the two.

Secret #27 – In word of mouth, any perceived attempt to influence the content can totally invalidate the communication program. If you do anything that smells or looks like trying to influence the content of word of mouth, such as bribes, kickbacks, etc., it will backfire and actually invalidate any good will you're attempting to create. In fact, if you have the superior product, influencing the content of its word of mouth is totally unnecessary. Just structure your messages to work with the experts to properly sequence and present their findings.

Secret #28 –The usual rules of advertising and salesmanship are often counterproductive to word-of-mouth marketing. Word of mouth operates by a completely different set of rules from advertising and sales. Word of mouth is a "live" medium.

The conventional wisdom of emphasizing the positive and moving towards the "close," dramatizing or hyping the benefits, advocacy language, and dozens of the other tried and true techniques used in sales and ads just don't apply to word of mouth. They will, in fact, destroy it.

Word-of-mouth marketing requires sensitivity to the goals and a special set of skills that are usually not found in advertising, sales training, promotion, and PR agencies.

For more, read *The Secrets of Word-of-Mouth Marketing: How to Trigger Exponential Sales Through Runaway Word of Mouth* AMACOM © 2001, George Silverman, President & Founder, Market Navigation, Inc., Orangeburg, NY. http://www.mnav.com

Bonus #2:

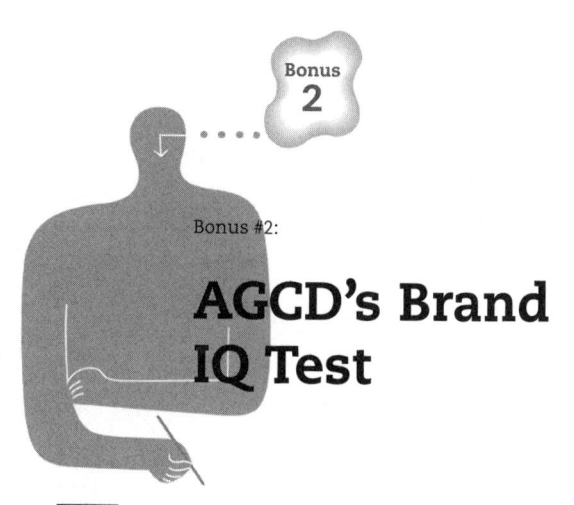

AGCD's Brand IQ Test

Think your brand is in great shape? Successful marketing is a function of the six pertinent P words...

Positioning

Packaging

Promotion

Persistence

Persuasion

Performance

Here's a quick and easy self-assessment test to see how you're doing in these six critical areas that are important to connecting with your potential customers, developing a distinctive identity, and realizing market leadership.

Score yourself from 0 to 5 points, with 5 being highest, on each of the questions. Subtotal each section, and then add up the subtotals for an overall score.

Positioning   Score (0–5)

1. You have developed a finely honed, clearly articulated, and emotionally meaningful solution statement that tells consumers what problem you address and what solution you can provide.

                                                                        Score_____

2. You know who your ideal customer is and exactly what they value as most important about the ideal product or service in your category.

                                                                        Score_____

3. You have studied and outlined a number of customer-centric benefits that your prospects can realize as a result of using your products and/or services.

                                                                        Score_____

4. You have a Unique Strategic Articulation that clarifies why your brand is different than all your competitors and why that's meaningful to your prospective customer.

                                                                        Score_____

5. Your brand will be pigeonholed by prospective customers. You are clear about the unique qualities you offer and what prospects and present customers perceive about these unique qualities.

                                                                        Score_____

                                                                        Subtotal_____

Packaging   Score (0–5)

6. You have an attractive, identifiable, appropriate, and distinctive "brand identity" that is carried through all your marketing materials.

Score_____

7. All your communications are presented as a value to the consumer. You can always answer their questions: "Why should I? What's in it for me?"

Score_____

8. What you do and how you do it, are clearly presented in brochures, ads, marketing packages, Web sites, etc. It's no mystery what the customer gets.

Score_____

9. You have a well-defined pricing strategy and a method for disseminating this information.

Score_____

10. Everything about your brand—from its logo, to packaging, to point of sale, to your office decor, even the way the receptionist answers the telephone—is presented in a way that supports your brand's positioning.

Score_____

Subtotal_____

Promotion   **Score (0–5)**

11. Through all your promotional vehicles, people get a sense of your product's personality and what its true value is.

                                                                        Score_____

12. You have several ways to actively generate referrals from existing customers. Word-of-mouth ("the buzz") is one of your strongest sources of new customers.

                                                                       Score_____

13. You stay visible to your target market(s) and expand your credibility through creatively provocative media advertising and public relations.

                                                                       Score_____

14. You communicate your expertise to your target audiences through speaking to groups and writing/publishing educational articles.

                                                                       Score_____

15. You send information to clients and prospects on a regular basis through a newsletter, e-zine or other means.

                                                                       Score_____

                                                                      Subtotal_____

Persistence   Score (0–5)

16. You have done your competitive homework and have up-to-date knowledge of their sales and marketing strategies and messages.

Score_____

17. You have made a commitment to using branding communications as a tool to fuel your brand's growth and maintain its vitality.

Score_____

18. You have a thorough knowledge of your ideal customer's spending habits, tastes, and what motivates them to buy.

Score_____

19. You have a process for establishing a marketing and communications budget that's adequate enough to remain visible and competitive.

Score_____

20. You have a clearly articulated brand communications policy and a system in place to ensure that policy is adhered to.

Score_____

Subtotal_____

Persuasion   Score (0–5)

21. Whenever you speak to someone about your brand you are totally focused on what you can do for them—how you can help them.

Score_____

22. You are skilled at building rapport by learning the past and present situation of your prospects through a series of well-thought-out questions.

Score_____

23. You are skilled at motivating customers to use your brand's offerings by discovering what values and benefits are the most important to them.

Score_____

24. You have a well-structured and well-organized presentation designed to inform prospects about exactly how you can solve their problems and meet their objectives.

Score_____

25. You're successful in asking for the business. You know what to say and do to win a prospect's commitment to your brand.

Score_____

Subtotal_____

Performance   Score (0–5)

26. You understand that the key to successful customer engagements is clear communication, and your company works constantly at improving this skill.

Score_____

27. Your brand makes clear, unambiguous promises: what it will deliver and what results the customer can expect. Your word is your bond—and you always keep it.

Score_____

28. When you make requests of customers, they are crystal-clear so that they know how to realize the best value from your product. They value you as a partner in their success.

Score_____

29. You stay motivated and true to your brand's vision and resist compulsive changes that can confuse customers and erode your brand's equity.

Score_____

30. You don't just offer a good product. You do everything in your power to exceed the customer's expectations and make it ludicrous for him to consider an alternative.

Score_____

Subtotal_____

Total Score (of a possible 150)_____

Interpreting your score

Over 130 points. You've got a great Brand IQ! Keep doing what you're doing well and pay some attention to the problem areas to realize even more market leadership.

101–130 points. The problem areas need serious attention. Address these now to prevent competitors from hurting your market position.

76–100 points. You need to make a commitment to understanding your audience and to align your brand with their needs. Developing a better product story, a more distinguishable brand articulation, and a sound value proposition will take an investment of funds, patience, and creative thinking before you will begin to realize market leadership.

50–75 points. Business is probably not that great. You're going to need help—and fast—to start turning things around.

Below 50 points. You have an identity crisis. You need to take a good look at exactly who you are and what you stand for before taking actions towards building your brand.

© 2002 AGCD. All rights reserved.

Appendix B

Resources for learning more

Recommended Reads:

Reading and learning from the info-gurus who eat, sleep, and breathe marketing communications (along with practicing what you learn) is key to your journey towards market leadership. Here are a few that I'd recommend. You can order most of them at a discount directly from Amazon.com.

Purple Cow
> Seth Godin

Seth explains our shift from the "TV industrial complex" to the information age and why it's ever so important in our market economy to find a way to make your business remarkable like a Purple Cow.

Selling the Invisible
> Harry Beckwith

Harry is right on the money with his lovely, easy-to-read-and-understand book about selling and marketing the intangible products of a service business. But his wisdom and logic apply even to folks selling a "touchy-feely" hard product as well.

Rapid Response Advertising
Geoff Ayling

I loved this book. Breaks new ground and illuminates new pathways to the mind of the consumer. It's honest, funny, well written, teeming with anecdotes, and fraught with revolutionary ideas.

The Fall of Advertising and the Rise of PR
Al Ries and Laura Ries

The father-and-daughter authors who previously collaborated on *The 22 Immutable Laws of Branding* here attempt to explain the difference between advertising and public relations, arguing the strengths of good PR and the "buzz" to launch new brands.

Raving Fans: A Revolutionary Approach to Customer Service
Ken Blanchard, Harvey Mackay, Sheldon Bowles

Written in the parable style of *The One Minute Manager*, *Raving Fans* uses a brilliantly simple and charming story to teach how to define a vision, learn what a customer really wants, institute effective systems, and make Raving Fan Service a constant feature—not just another program of the month.

Positioning: The Battle for Your Mind
Al Ries and Jack Trout

The classic book that changed the way people market their products and services. Describes creating a "position" in a prospective customer's mind—one that reflects a company's own strengths and weaknesses as well as those of its competitors. Also read other books by Jack Trout or Al Ries.

Ogilvy on Advertising
    David Ogilvy

A must-have in any marketer's library. A candid and indispensable primer on all aspects of advertising from the man Time has called "the most sought-after wizard in the business."

Why People Don't Buy Things
    Harry Washburn and Kim Wallace

Using proven, field-tested techniques, the authors break down the customer's buying decision in a step-by-step fashion and show you how to identify different buyer's profiles.

A New Brand World
    Scott Bedbury, Stephen Fenichell

How did a company like Nike use "Just Do It" to launch its way to success and become part of global culture? How did Starbucks reinvent a familiar nine-hundred-year-old product and change the way people drink coffee around the world? Bedbury, who worked at both companies, gives the inside scoop on really differentiating yourself and commanding a premium price.

Smart Things to Know About Brands & Branding
John L. Mariotti
Understand how to capitalize on the power of brands. The author describes what you need to know as a manager and provides a framework for practical action.

Good to Great: Why Some Companies Make the Leap and Others Don't
Jim Collins
A fascinating detailed research study, author Collins explores the factors that make the difference between great brands that endure and shooting stars that quickly burn out.

How to Become a Marketing Superstar: Unexpected Rules That Ring the Cash Register
Jeffrey J. Fox
A great primer on marketing packed with common sense and practical advice for business managers and marketers. Throughout, Jeff never loses sight of what he sees as marketing's ultimate goal, the super marketer's anthem: *It don't mean a thing, if it don't go ka-ching!*"

99% Inspiration: Tips, Tales & Techniques for Liberating Your Business Creativity
Bryan W. Mattimore
Bryan is a brainstorming genius. I've been in groups led by him and they've been fun and exhilarating. Bryan shares stories and teaches you great techniques for breaking any creative logjam.

Some Helpful Web Sites

The Internet is packed with valuable information and resources for building your brand to leadership. Here are some to check out. Some are web focused, others are business focused, and many are just about marketing principles and strategies. All have solid content about marketing that you can apply.

www.actionplan.com
The site of Robert Middleton. Info-guru, mentor, coach, and marketing consultant to independent professionals who want to attract more clients. Sign up for Robert's weekly newsletter—it's great!

www.allaboutbranding.com
A "satellite" site of dna design out of New Zealand. Comprehensive library of information related to marketing, shaping, and enriching your understanding of brands.

www.aweber.com
Set up auto responder messages. Someone downloads something from your Web site; they automatically get fed messages at staged intervals. Messages can be personalized to each recipient. A great timesaving way to stay in touch.

www.brandingdiva.com
Karen Post "The Branding Diva": speaker, author, marketing-communications, branding consultant with over twenty years experience of helping organizations and individuals achieve more through their "Landed Brand." Sign up for her free *Brain Tattoo* e-zine.

www.buildingbrands.com
BuildingBrands.com focuses on brands, branding, marketing and communications. It includes original articles, interactive learning games and also offers a free *Shared Learning* newsletter.

www.ecnow.com
A collection of the most important strategies for marketing on the Internet.

www.guru.com
A resource for gurus and professional service businesses. Lots of articles on marketing and running your business.

www.lmca.net
Have an established brand? LMCA can show you how to profit from your brand's equity through licensing your trade name. (An AGCD client, by the way.)

www.marcommwise.com
Services, information, book reviews, etc., on marketing-related topics.

www.mnav.com
Home of George Silverman (author of *The Secrets of Word of Mouth Marketing*). Market Navigation conducts research and consults to help you find better ways of accelerating the customer's decision making process, primarily through harnessing word of mouth.

www.MarketingProfs.com
A great source for articles and information on marketing your business.

www.pertinent.com/articles/marketing/index.asp
A whole lot of articles on a wide range of marketing topics—mostly for smaller businesses.

www.marketingpower.com
Official site of the American Marketing Association. News, suppliers, tools, and info for marketers. Sign up for their *Marketing Power* newsletter, too.

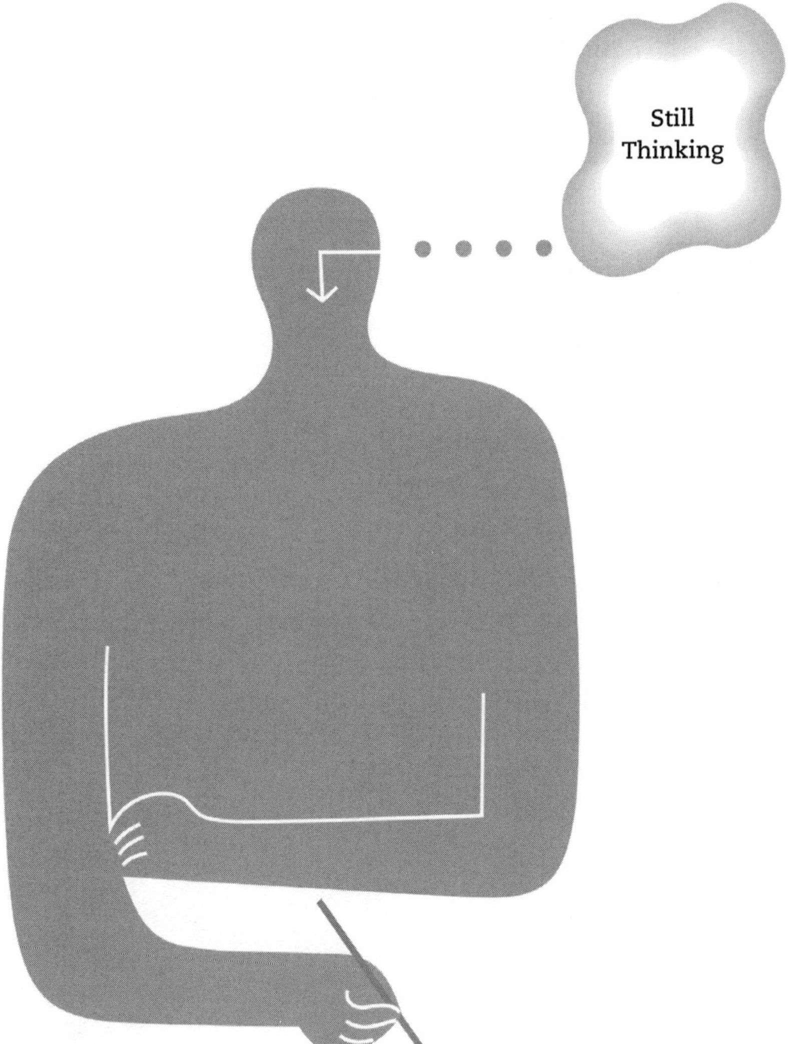
Still
Thinking

Find out more. Sign up for our newsletter. Get a free report.

For more about brand building, to sign up for a subscription to the *Briefs for Building Better Brands* newsletter and to download the free report "Ten Marketing Secrets for Building a Sexier Brand" please visit our corporate site at www.agcd.com or call us at (973) 509-2715.

Get more copies of this book at quantity discount prices.

Additional copies of this book are available through online booksellers such as Amazon.com and BN.com. Discounts are available when ordered in quantity for bulk purchases and special sales. Please call us at (973) 509–2715 or send an e-mail to Bebe Landis, bsl@brandspa-llc.com with your inquiry.

Write or e-mail Allan Gorman

We'd love to hear from you with any comments and/or questions pertaining to market leadership; or if there are any topics you think you'd like to see in future issues of *Briefs for Building Better Brands,* please write or send an e-mail to Allan Gorman, agorman@brandspa-llc.com.

To discuss private consultation, or to get information about Mr. Gorman speaking to your group, contact us and schedule an exploratory chat.

> **AGCD**
> Market Leadership Advisors
> 215 Glenridge Avenue,
> Montclair, NJ 07042
> (973) 509–2715
>
> Send an e-mail to: agorman@brandspa-llc.com

Visit http://www.brandspa-llc.com
for books, free white papers, CDs and other merchandise

Allan Gorman is owner and chief creative officer of AGCD, a Montclair, New Jersey, firm that specializes in helping clients realize market leadership.

An authority on branding and strategic communications, he's written dozens of articles and white papers on the subject and produces similar discussions in a monthly online e-zine—*Briefs for Building Better Brands*.

A thirty-plus-year veteran of the advertising and design communications industry, Gorman has served in senior creative capacities for many major advertising agencies in New York and New Jersey, working on some of the world's most successful brands. Gorman first attended, then taught at the School of Visual Arts in New York City and studied movie-making at NYU's School of Film. His creative talent has been cited and showcased in *Graphic Design: USA* and *Adweek*, as well as in numerous weekly and monthly publications; and he has been the recipient of over four hundred industry accolades and awards.

To download the free report: *Ten Marketing Secrets for Building a Sexier Brand*, or to have Mr. Gorman speak to your group, visit www.agcd.com, or call Bebe Landis at (973) 509-2728.

Index

99% Inspiration, 6

A
Action Plan Marketing, 4
ad agencies, 66
ad community, 67
Advantage Builder Services, 5
advertisement, 68
advertising, 28, 67, 119, 124
advertising themes, 59
Adweek ,4, 143
AGCD, 137
AGCD Brandspa™ Books, 144
Amazon.com, 140
American Marketing Association, 136
animal hospital, 43
appeal to his emotions, 30
appeals, 55
art of branding, 53
audio logo, 82, 83
auto responder ,134
award-caliber creative, 68
Ayling, Geoff, 58, 131

B
bad experience, 86
bad perception, 86
Baker, David C., 6
basis for repeat business, 26
Becker, Professor Sandy, 17
Beckett & Beckett, 4
Beckwith, Harry, 130
becoming famous, 35
becoming THAT!, 51
Big Apple, 24
big idea, 40
Blanchard, Ken, 131
blitz, 112
BN.com, 140
board think, 38
bonus check, 62
bouncers, 27
Bowles, Sheldon, 131
bragging, 34
Brain Tattoo, 3, 135
brainstorm, 55
brand, 35, 87
Brand IQ Test, 121
brand articulation, 52
brand distinction, 47
brand experience, 100, 104
brand identity, 123
brand is your story, 53
brand mission, 49
brand story, 54, 68, 70
brand-building ,59
branding, 22, 33, 34, 47, 96, 97

Branding Diva, the, 135
branding takes action, 35
branding takes
    being unique, 34
branding takes bragging, 34
brandspa, 151
brandspa-llc, 151
Briefs for Building
    Better Brands, 72, 137, 143, 151
Brooklyn, N.Y., 47
business customers, 96
buy low/ sell high
    marketing strategy, 20
buying decision, 98
buzz, 67

C

cashews, 85
Celebrity *Mercury*, 22
changing your message, 40
charismatic brand, 58, 59
Chihuahua, 59
Christmas, 64
Christmas bonus, 61
classify and pigeonhole ,27
Coca-Cola Company, 73
commodity, 80, 83
Conde Nast Traveler, 23
Consult Ad Hoc Inc., 4
Conversation Arts Media, 5
core marketing message, 39
core value proposition, 39

corporate culture, 62
corporate identity, 92
creating delight, 23
creating more customers, 20
Croda Inc., 11
customer's expectations, 46
customers, 55, 112
CVP, 39, 40

D

Dawkins, Richard, 58
decision makers, 113
decision to buy process, 113
decision-making process, 110
definition of a brand, 53
delight, 53
design, 77
develop a clear identity, 29
direct marketing, 108
distinguish your brand, 70
distributors, 55
Diva, 24
dna design 134

E

Eastwick Colleges, 12
elevator speech, 52
emotion, 28
emotional "whys", 41
employee, 62
endorsements, 116
Energizer Bunny, 40

excellence and service, 56
experience, 53
experience of the product, 53
expert influencers, 114
experts, 115

F
Fall of Advertising and the Rise of PR, The, 131
Fancy Foods Trade Show, 85
Father Christmas, 73
flowers, 64
focus groups, 56
foolproof approach, 41
former customers, 55
formula, 84
Fox, Jeffrey J., 5
fun, 61

G
Gabor, Don, 5
Gayle Turner, 4
Gen-X, Gen-Y, 17
Gilbert, Dr. Rob, 100
Godin, Seth, 130
good design, 76
Gorman, Allan, 143, 151
Gorman—One on One number One, 151
Graphic Design: USA, 143
graphic designer, 80

H
Have it your way,. 59
help him recall your name, 30
homework, 54
HOW Magazine, 6
How To Become a Rainmaker, 5
How to Start a Conversation and Make Friends, 5

I
IC&C, Inc., 6
ideas, 39
Identity, 27
IKEA, 68
imitation, 74
information age, 130
Inner Circle of Choices Club, 25
internal audit, 55
IQ Test, 121

J
Jacob Javitts Exhibition Center, 85
Jersey City Medical Center, 12
Jones, Tom, 4
Just Do It!, 59

K
K. Hovnanian Companies, 12
kill off your brand, 40

146

L

Landed Brand, 135
Landis, Bebe, 137
Levinson, Jay Conrad, 3
lifeblood of your business, 52
Lippincott Mercer, 5
LMCA, 12, 135
logo, 52, 59
lone star state, 86
loyalty, 68
Lynch, Liz, 4

M

Mackay, Harvey, 131
Madison Avenue, 51
Manhattan Bridge, 47
market leader, 72, 78
market leaders, 24
Market leadership, 39, 89
Market Leadership Advisors, 141
market research, 29, 56
market-test, 55
marketing, 28, 33, 52, 82
marketing briefs, 32
marketing guru, 51
Marketing Mastery, 51
marketing medium, 71
marketing plans, 89

Mattimore, Bryan, 6
maximize profitability mindset, 20
meme, 58
Mercury, 22
Middleton, Robert, 4, 51, 151
Montclair, 24
Montclair State University, 100

N

names, 52
negative remarks, 118
networking, 116
New York, 85
nightclub, 24
NJ Skyline, 85
noise barrier, 30
NYC subway, 47
NYU, 137

O

offer a benefit, 30
one and only, 39
one-man operation, 56
Order form, 152
original identity, 72
Orp man, 47, 48
out of the box thinking, 21

P

packaging, 121, 123
penetrate his "noise" barrier, 30
performance, 121, 127
persistence, 121, 125
persuasion, 121, 126
Peters, Dennis, 3
Phillips, Eliot, 5
pigeonhole, 29
Pink Bunny, 59
planning, 38
positioning, 51, 57, 121, 122
positioning your product
 or service properly, 51
*Positioning: The Battle for
 Your Mind*, 131
Post, Karen, 3, 135
power of brand experience, 100
PR firm, 66
press coverage, 68
Price, Scott, 85
pricing strategy, 123
process of discovery, 41
procrastinating, 32
professionalism, 79
promoting and selling, 33
promotion, 121, 124
prospects, 55
public relations, 67, 116, 124
Purple Cow, 130
putting off your marketing, 32

R

*Rapid Response
 Advertising*, 58, 131
raving fan, 23
*Raving Fans: A Revolutionary
 Approach to
 Customer Service*, 131
real core message, 41
recall, 28, 53
ReCourses, Inc., 6
referrals, 116
research, 54, 70
resentment, 28
return on your investment, 71
Ries, Al, 3, 131
Ries, Laura, 66, 131
Roche Pharmaceuticals, 12
Rooney, Linda C., 5
Rutgers, 17

S

Santa, 72
School of Visual Arts, 143
scientific method, 54
self-Interest, 28
self-replicating idea, 58
selling, 109
Selling the Invisible, 130
sequence, 113
Shared Learning, 135
Silverman, George, 108, 136
Sisti & Others, 6

Sisti, Michael A., 6
St. Nick, 73
St. Patrick, 73
Starbucks, 68
strong brand, 53, 97
subway, 47
Sundblom, Haddon, 73
system, 29

T
tag line, 52, 59
talking louder, 34
Ten Marketing Secrets for Building a Sexier Brand, 143, 151
Texas, 85
The Growth Engine Co., 6
Inner Circle of Choices Club, 26, 77
The Secrets of Word-of-Mouth Marketing, 108
Think Different, 59
third-party endorsements, 67
Tourette Syndrome Association, 12
trade show, 92
trickle-down effect, 115
Trout, Jack, 131
TV industrial complex, 130

U
Unique Strategic Articulation, 122

V
value proposition, 67
values statement, 89
vet, 43
viral marketing, 40
vision, 89
visual message, 92
Volkswagen, 61

W
Watson, Gary, 6
Weinstein, Matt, 63
What's in it for me?, 80
word-of-mouth, 124
word-of-mouth marketing, 108
Work Like Your Dog—50 ways to Work Less, Play More and Earn More, 63
world's leading brands, 41

Y
Yellow Pages, 80

Z
Ziggy 43

You might also enjoy these offerings from AGCD Brandspa Books...

Ten Marketing Secrets for Building a Sexier Brand

Allan Gorman addresses a Graduate Chapter of the American Marketing Association at Montclair State University.

Ten Secrets reveals:
- The difference between sales and marketing
- Techniques you can start using now to differentiate yourself
- How to win customers in tough economic times, and more.

(CD-ROM—51 min., 34 sec.) Item # AG 121a **$10.95**

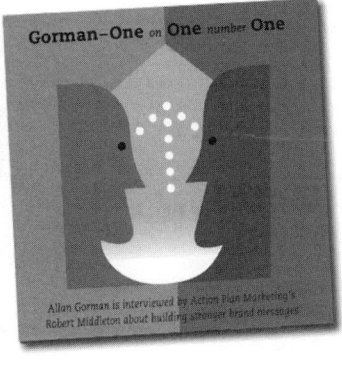

Gorman—One *on* One *number* One.

Gorman has a lively discussion about branding with Action Plan Marketing's Robert Middleton.

Their in-depth talk reveals even more insights into what it takes to develop a distinct and attractive brand story that can set you apart and help you attract better and more lucrative customers.

(CD-ROM—1 hr., 5 min.) Item # AG 111a
$8.95

Use the order form on the other side of this page and check our website: www.brandspa-llc.com for more

AGCD Brandspa™ Books Quick Order Form

Fax orders: Dial 973-509-2678 (Send this completed form).

Phone orders: Call 800 981 AGCD (2423) toll free.
(Leave a message and we'll call you back ASAP.)

e-mail orders: orders@brandspa-llc.com

Mail orders: AGCD Brandspa Books; 215 Glenridge Ave.; Montclair, NJ 07042; Phone: 973 509 2715

Please send me the following books, disks or other merchandise. *I understand that I may return any of them for a full refund within 30 days—no questions asked.*

_____

_____

_____

Please send me Free information about:
- ☐ Other Books and CDs   ☐ Speaking/Seminars
- ☐ Workshops/Consulting   ☐ Add my name to the e-zine list

Name _____
Address _____
City _____ State _____ Zip _____
Phone _____
e-mail _____

Sales tax: Add 6% State Sales Tax for orders shipped to NJ.

Shipping and handling: US orders: Add $4.00 for the first book and $2.00 for each additional product. **International:** Add $10.00 for the first book and $4.00 for each additional product.

Payment Info:
- ☐ Check (mail orders only)   ☐ Visa   ☐ Mastercard
- ☐ AMEX   ☐ Discover   Sorry, no COD payments.

For quantity orders, call for a discount schedule

Card #_____ Exp _____
Address _____
Name of cardholder _____
Signature _____

Give us some feedback on the book you read (optional) _____
_____
_____